Endorsements

Being "in the world but not of the world"—what exactly does that mean? And, more importantly, just what does that look like in our culture today? In *Live Full, Walk Free* Cindy Bultema takes us on a fact-finding excursion to the ancient city of Corinth. Here we unearth a physical landscape that looks very different from ours yet a moral climate that almost mirrors what we witness today—temptations at every turn, immorality run wild—even idolatry. People overindulging in pleasure, leading often to sin, as they undervalue the warnings and commands laid out for us in Scripture. This spiritually helpful book knits some of Cindy's personal experience into an insightful study of 1 Corinthians as it provides practical strategies for carefully walking in today's world without stepping into sin.

—**Karen Ehman**, Proverbs 31 Ministries speaker; *New York Times* bestselling author of *Keep It Shut* and *Listen, Love, Repeat*; wife; and mother of three

Cindy beautifully weaves her story of healing and transformation with Paul's revolutionary letter to the Corinthian church. Her passionate and winsome teaching unfolds the life-changing biblical truths that freed her from a life of drug addiction and promiscuity. Through Scripture and personal stories, Cindy shares practical ways to align your heart with God's Word and creative ways to apply that Word so you live confidently, fully, and freely in this immoral, crazy, mixed-up world.

—**Wendy Blight**, Member of Proverbs 31 Ministries' First 5 Writing Team, speaker, Bible teacher, and author of *I Know His Name*, *Living So That*, and *Hidden Joy in a Dark Corner*

live full WALK FREE

A Journey through 1 CORINTHIANS

SET APART in a SIN-SOAKED WORLD

CINDY BULTEMA

THOMAS NELSON
Since 1798

Published in Nashville, Tennessee, by Thomas Nelson. Thomas Nelson is a registered trademark of HarperCollins Christian Publishing, Inc.

Thomas Nelson titles may be purchased in bulk for educational, business, fund-raising, or sales promotional use. For information, please e-mail SpecialMarkets@ ThomasNelson.com.

Page design and layout: CrosslinCreative.net
Images: VectorStock, ClipArt.co

ISBN: 978-0-310-08209-5

 Dedication

To Julie Richardson—

Who would have ever guessed where our
walking path would lead us?

Thank you for inspiring me to turn my passions into prayer,
and modeling what it means to truly listen and wait on God.

I'll treasure your friendship forever.

A sweet friendship refreshes the soul.
—Proverbs 27:9 MSG

Acknowledgments

With a grateful heart, I thank my beloved friends and family:

My powerful prayer team—Thank you for "praying down the tracks" every step of the way. Your prayers and love make all the difference. How I thank God for you . . . again and again!

My beloved "Guinea Pigs"—Thank you for secretly going through all the lessons and sharing your feedback, encouragement, and wisdom. You truly were "God's provision" to me.

Mary S.—You inspire me to follow hard after Jesus. Thanks for sharing your love, life, coffee, and handouts. I promise to never stop "giving them meat."

Robin P.—Who knew where a random meeting on an elevator could lead us? *Only God!* Thanks for your support, pep talks, and love. I'm super thankful our families are "fwends."

Sally B.—Your wisdom, counsel, and daily phone calls have been lifesavers to me. Thanks for always telling me what you really think. Everyone needs a Sally in their life.

My friends at Sunshine Community Church and Tabernacle Community Church in Grand Rapids, Michigan—Thank you for hosting opportunities to share and shape these messages!

Autee—Thanks for being awesome, servant-hearted, coffee-getting you! You are a gift!

Lorilee, my talented writing coach—Thanks for reminding me to make my words sizzle!

Paulette—Thanks for your wisdom and praying for my tsunami. Cindy B. loves you.

My new friends from the New York School of the Bible—We loved touring Greece with you!

My parents, Don and Ramona—Thank you for your unconditional love and grace, and for not giving up on me, ever. I am who I am because of your support, even in my darkest days.

My in-laws, Bob and Jackie—Your practical gifts of help, encouragement, and support mean so very much! Can you bring us coffee ice cream pie every day?

My guy John—Thanks for living this message with me. I love you. #Corinth2016

My gang: Jake, Benj, Manda, and Sarah—Being your mom is one of my greatest delights, and I love you more than you'll ever know. Thank you for letting me share our everyday stories.

To the incredible team at HarperCollins Christian Publishing—Thank you for your wisdom, counsel, investment, and support. I'm humbled to serve alongside of you.

Sweet Jesus, all of my days I want to praise You! Jesus, it's all for You.

Contents

How to Use This Study

Welcome to *Live Full, Walk Free!* I'm super excited you have chosen to join me on this adventure through 1 Corinthians. Together, let's journey to ancient Corinth and travel with Paul to the "Sin City" of his day as we seek to learn how to best cultivate a pure life in our impure world. Whether you have been studying the Bible for decades or are still trying to figure this "Jesus thing" out, you'll find Paul's letter to the church of Corinth—and us today—will meet us right where we are on our spiritual journey.

To get started, you'll need a few supplies: a Bible, this *Live Full, Walk Free* book, the teaching videos (optional), and community.

⚜ **Bible:** I mainly teach from the New International Version, but if you don't own this translation, you'll be able to complete the lessons without difficulty. In fact, using various translations will enrich your learning. Let's dig into God's Word so that we might *know* Truth, *live* Truth, and *share* Truth with others.

⚜ ***Live Full, Walk Free* book:** Each lesson includes three parts: an introduction, a section for "Digging Deeper" in God's Word, and "Apply It"—a chance for you to put the truths into practice in your own life. Although the lesson lengths vary, you should be able to complete each one within 20–30 minutes. Go at your own pace; there's grace!

Together, we'll be highlighting many key passages from the book of 1 Corinthians. We won't have time to explore every verse, so I would encourage you to dive into 1 Corinthians on your own and fully explore all sixteen chapters. For this very purpose, I've included a reading guide at the back of this book, breaking the letter into bite-sized pieces.

You'll also be invited to memorize six new Bible verses—one each week. One of my favorite Scripture memory tips is putting the verse on an index card and keeping it right by the bathroom sink. We may get busy, but we usually brush our teeth, right? You'll also note the verses are printed for you at the back of this book.

❀ **Teaching videos:** A *Live Full, Walk Free* six-session video series is available in both DVD and downloadable formats (sold separately). Although the videos aren't a requirement, I highly recommend them. Each session provides additional teaching on 1 Corinthians, with themes including: identity, unity, purity, and purpose. You'll find the messages enhance the material in your book and are pretty fun too. (When was the last time you saw women dressed as a drunken sailor, slave, and Roman soldier in your Bible study teaching?) If you or your group choose to utilize the video teachings, be sure to complete the book chapter *before* watching the video.

You'll also find a free bonus introductory video on the DVD. I wanted to start our time together by sharing openly and honestly my own journey of faith with you. For many years, I lived an empty, self-defeating, rebellious lifestyle. Until the amazing day Jesus set me free! The good news is: if He can do it for me, He can do it for you too! There's no one too far gone from God's amazing grace.

❀ **Community:** *Live Full, Walk Free* can be read individually or with a small group. I highly recommend a group setting, such as a neighborhood Bible study, Sunday school class, office lunch hour get-together, or other small group gathering. I believe life change happens in community! After viewing the video teaching together, members will participate in a group discussion. Ideally, discussion groups should be no larger than eight to ten people. If your group is larger, you may want to watch the video together, and then break into smaller groups to encourage sharing from everyone. Discussion questions are included. You'll also find additional free small group helps at www.cindybultema.com.

Lastly, the *Live Full, Walk Free* curriculum is a tool, but the ultimate goal is helping women grow closer to Jesus in the context of a welcoming, safe, and fun environment. For that reason, *Live Full, Walk Free* is designed to be informative yet adaptable. If you are a brand new group, you may want more time in the beginning getting to know one another. If the women in your group are new to God's Word, you may want extra time examining the Scriptures. Shape the study to what best suits the needs and desires of your individual group.

Let's start our adventure by getting to know one another. Gather your supplies, grab some girlfriends, and start a *Live Full, Walk Free* gathering! After you get acquainted with your group members, I'll share a bit of my faith story in the introductory video lesson. Don't forget to introduce yourself to me too. Why not take a quick "before" photo of your group and email it to cindy@cindybultema.com? I'd love to meet you!

I'm so glad to walk with you, friend. Let the journey begin!

Message from Cindy

One of my first memories as a little girl, growing up in small-town Indiana, was crouching under my dad's desk and turning the pages of his *Playboy* magazines in wonder. These ladies were so pretty—I was in awe of them and their perfect, Barbie doll bodies. I was just three years old, and looking at those magazines planted a seed in me: I wanted to grow up and look like that.

Another memory dates back to when I was around four or five. As we'd drive down a populated main street not far from our house, my eyes would linger on the risqué night club positioned on the corner. From the darkness outside, I could see the women dancing seductively on the tables. I could see their bodies silhouetted, dark against the red lights of the tavern. Again, another seed was planted: I wanted to be like those mysterious, shadowy ladies someday. It was obvious to me that they were the epitome of beauty.

A few years later, when I was still a little girl, I would stick a poster on my wall of the Dallas Cowboy cheerleaders—curvy, gorgeous, and just like the ladies in those *Playboy* magazines, but with more clothes on. One more time, it was a symbol of my hoped-for future.

That was all I knew.

* * *

In ancient Corinth, a little girl would have seen just as much as I saw, except she would have seen naked women—and men—up close and in person. She would have watched as parades celebrating the deities marched by, featuring floats with giant phalluses and couples having sex.

She would have thought it was normal that her mommy and daddy went to worship at the temple of Aphrodite, the goddess of love. She would not have blinked to see prostitutes walking by her house, their shoes stamped with the Greek words for "Follow Me." As a matter of routine, that little Corinthian girl would have seen men kissing men, and women kissing women. It was like that Taylor Swift song, "Welcome to New York": "Boys with boys, girls with girls: Welcome to New York." Two thousand years ago, the lyrics could easily have been, "Boys with boys, girls with girls. Welcome to Corinth." In fact, New York pales in comparison to Corinth. Nearly every place in our modern world does.

I am pretty sure that little Corinthian girl's tender heart was planted with the same seeds as my own: *This is what I want to look like when I grow up. This is who I want to be.* Voluptuous, sensual, wanted. How do I know this? Because just like my own upbringing, her house, her family, her community was a kind of culture, a culture marked by immorality, idolatry, and indulgence. That was all she knew.

Corinth was the Sin City of its day, a locale so famously debauched that the saying went *"non licet omnibus adire Corinthum"*: "Not everyone is able to go to Corinth." In other words, you better be a hardcore sinner to be able to handle this level of wickedness.

It was in this setting, this culture that Paul chose to live for eighteen months—a whole year and a half! That's no casual visit, and it certainly wasn't a blissful Grecian vacation. Paul came to live among and establish the church in Corinth because they desperately needed it. He knew the place, its vices and temptations very well. He knew exactly what the church members were facing every day there—the nonstop bad behavior, fanaticism for false gods, and wild excesses.

So later, when he wrote the epic letter to his friends in Corinth, it seems obvious what would be inside when they un-scrolled his words:

Run! Pack up your families, pets, and belongings and make a mad dash for the next town, where things are (a bit) better!

If you have to stay, try to keep far, far away from your sinful friends and neighbors. Associate only with other Christians, and pull your shades at night. You should be fine, in that case.

But really, if you can, run!

But that's not what he said. When the church members read the words of their letter, Paul had a different message for them. Oh, he said a lot of things to them—strong things, corrections for the way they had been living in Sin City. They had bought into the common lies and deceptions of their culture, and were living out those false beliefs. The church members had left their hearts, bodies, and minds unguarded, and therefore had sunk into deep and damaging compromise. They had forgotten their new identities in Christ, and forsaken grace and life-bringing freedom. They had blown it and messed up big time in Sin City.

Isn't it compelling, though, that Paul doesn't command them to move, run, or hide in their cozy, churchy bunkers?

Nope—he basically tells them to do the opposite: Be a Christian *where you are. Live* victoriously and winsomely among the porn magazines, the lascivious, the shocking, the lewd, while not *participating* in these things. *Live* winningly among the temple prostitutes, the vulgar parade floats, the idol worship, while not *joining* in these activities. Stay and live, not like those who have no hope, but like those who do. Live like those who have *so much* hope.

And most of all, don't live in bondage as slaves to sin but as slaves to Christ. Live with abundance, in the fullness of your identity in Christ. Live and walk with freedom!

I must admit—this sounds fantastic, but part of me balks at this. *How* can we live free in such imprisoned surroundings? *How* do we live full lives in a culture polluted through and through?

This is the question I want us to explore within the pages of this book. How?

We're not the first people to ask these questions or have this struggle, and we're definitely not the first to live in Sin City. The Corinthians asked the same question: How? And the answers lie in the truth of Paul's letter to this struggling, flailing, messed-up group of people. What he reveals in this letter changes everything—for our brothers and sisters two thousand years ago, and for us today. This letter shows us the truth, and we've never needed it so badly before.

So let's dig deep into the words of an ageless letter, because that letter was written to each one of us. We must learn to embrace our identity in Christ, walking in grace and life-bringing freedom. We must agree with Paul that yes, no matter how bad things look, there is a better way.

We have all we need to live fully and walk freely in this time and place. We have all we need, here and now, to be part of the solution and not the problem. We have all we need to cultivate holy, liberated lives, even in Sin City.

It's time friends. It's time!

Cindy ☺

Bonus Video Introduction:
CINDY'S STORY

Use the space below to note anything that stands out to you from the introductory video. You may also choose to take notes on a separate sheet of paper.

CHAPTER ONE

Welcome to Sin City

Prayer:

O God, how I thank You for fresh starts and new beginnings. I come before You eager and expectant to see what You have planned on this *Live Full, Walk Free* journey. Open my eyes, ears, heart, and mind to all You have prepared for me to learn through Your powerful, life-changing Word. Please remove any and all distractions that could get in the way of my time with You. Lord, I invite You to fill me anew with Your power and strength so that I might truly *live full* and *walk free*. I cannot wait to see what You will do. In the powerful, amazing name of Jesus I pray. Amen.

PART ONE:
Bridging the Gap

> **Memory Verse:** For the message of the cross is foolishness to those who are perishing, but to us who are being saved it is the power of God.
>
> —1 Corinthians 1:18

Hi friends! Are you ready to dig into Bible study? Isn't there something meaningful about Day One, Part One? I adore fresh starts, new gel pens, crisp white pages. And I love the expectation of eye-opening insights and revelations through God's Word!

What are you most looking forward to this season? In what areas of your life do you desire to live more fully and walk more freely? Are there obstacles that prevent you from experiencing all God has for you? Why not take a moment and record your thoughts inside the back cover of this *Live Full, Walk Free* book, and then join me for a road trip back to ancient Corinth.

By the way, my husband John and I did the Corinth road trip (air trip, actually) a few months ago, and I'm bursting with golden tidbits of what we saw firsthand in that captivating place that still yields bold and modern truths for us today. I want you to feel as if you are there with me—walking the paths where the Isthmian athletes trained, running your fingers over the limestone columns of the temple of Apollo, and inhaling air scented by the Gulf of Corinth, just as our brothers and sisters did two thousand years ago.

(Warning: This opening section may seem a teensy bit "educational," but hang with me, friend. Not every day will be as much history, I promise.)

Whenever we begin studying a book or section of the Bible, it's crucial—and fascinating—to gain an understanding of the original setting in which it was written. What was the society like? Are we talking about a big city or a quaint rural town? Were the people wealthy or poor, slaves or free? Since there are two millennia between us and these particular Corinthians, we are going to add time travel to our armchair travel experience. The better we really *get* their lives, culture, and times, the better we understand Paul's meaning, for them, *and for us*.

As we begin to un-scroll the book of 1 Corinthians, let's lean in and peek through the portal of time at Corinth, the Sin City of its day. Getting our bearings in Corinth will make our trek through this book all the more memorable.

For all my map-loving friends, here are some insights into the geography of the area to help you get oriented:

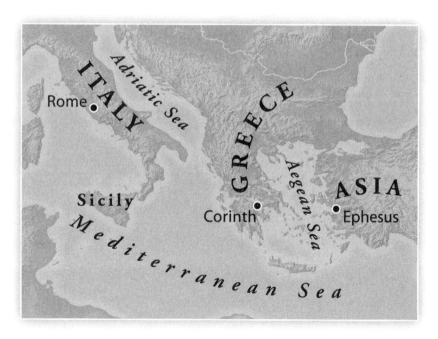

Beginning on the left, you'll see the boot of Italy, Greece in the center, and then ancient Asia Minor, present-day Turkey, on the far right.

City: Greece is divided into two parts—upper Greece and lower Greece, which is also known as the Peloponnese peninsula. Do you see the city of Corinth situated there in the middle? Corinth was located near a four-mile-wide isthmus which served as a land-bridge between the mainland of Greece and the Peloponnese region to the south.

Because of its strategic location with *two* active harbors, Corinth was one of the most bustling port cities of its day. Like the center of an hourglass, everything passed through Corinth.

Corinth's prime location fueled its prosperity and wealth, and made it a multicultural magnet. Tourists packed the place out, and spent money on lodging, food, and luxury products and services provided by a host of entrepreneurs. You could do some serious damage shopping in the market, picking up Arabian balsam, Phoenician dates, Libyan ivory, Babylonian carpets, Cilician goat's hair, and Lycaonian wool.[1] Sounds like Corinth made a fabulous place for a girlfriends' shopping getaway!

People: After a tumultuous history, Corinth was established as a Roman colony in 44 BC.[2] As an international trade center, Corinth was populated with mainly Romans, Greeks, and Jews; plus Syrians, Asians, and Egyptians too. It is estimated that in Paul's day 250,000 free persons and some 400,000 slaves called Corinth home, not to mention the thousands of tradesmen, sailors, and tourists who visited.[3]

 If we do the math, 250,000 + 400,000 = approximately _____ people from all over the known world made their home in Corinth.

 How does your city compare in size to Corinth? What nationalities and backgrounds make up your community?

Culture: We know Corinth was rich, with an economy humming like a well-oiled Bentley. It also had a serious reputation for illicit activities and behaviors. Anything went in Corinth—and I do mean *anything*. As we explore the city, consider three important words describing their culture: indulgent, idolatrous, and immoral.

🌼 **Indulgent:** Because of its wealth, Corinth became a city of luxury and lavishness. The affluent citizens developed an unapologetic love of possessions and pleasure. Overindulgence was the objective and pleasure the goal.

> *Anything went in Corinth— and I do mean anything.*

🌼 **Idolatrous:** In Corinth, gods and goddesses ruled, and religious expressions were incredibly varied. You could worship the assorted gods of Egypt, Rome, and Greece—your choice. There was the Jewish synagogue, plus temples, shrines, and statues on nearly every corner. Religious activities were part of everyday life, too. ("Honey, on your way home from worshiping Aphrodite, could you grab a pint of goat's milk?")

🌼 **Immoral:** Around the whole ancient world, Corinth acquired a reputation for depravity, wickedness, and filth. In the ancient Greek plays, if an actor was portraying a Corinthian citizen, he/she was usually drunk and recklessly involved with the Greek party life and prostitutes.

In fact, the term *Corinthian girl* meant "prostitute," and *korinthiazesthai*—to live like a Corinthian—meant to live with drunken and immoral depravity.[4] Sex was *everywhere*, in every shape, form, and perversion.

Were the Corinthians embarrassed about their sinful status? Oh no—the Corinthians were loud and proud about their reputation. Immorality was one of the city's most publicized attractions. Corinth's reputation implied that you were *going* to fall into damaging behaviors, and engage in activities that were secret, hidden, and shameful—it was expected and celebrated!

 In 1 Corinthians 6:9–10, Paul lists some of the specific sins for which the city was noted and which formerly described many believers in the Corinthian church. Record them below:

Indulgent. Idolatrous. Immoral. Yet in this hotbed of wickedness, the most unlikely place in all the Greek world, God was at work, preparing to shake things up in Sin City. An important visitor was on his way to Corinth, and this shame-soaked city would never be the same.

🌿 *Digging Deeper*

The apostle Paul, the first-century missionary God used to author 1–2 Corinthians, arrived in Corinth for the first time in approximately 51 AD. Do you think Paul had his work cut out for him as he sought to make a difference in this pagan, corrupt culture? Yes? Me too!

Let's dig into God's Word and refresh our memory regarding Paul's own journey from darkness to light.

 Read Acts 8:3, which records the first persecution of the early church. How is Saul (Saul is his Hebrew name, Paul is his Greek name) involved?

Read Acts 9:1–22, the first of three accounts of Saul's conversion to Christ.[5] What does Saul's transformation—from murderer of Christ followers to passionate messenger for Jesus—teach us about the nature of God?

In Acts 13:9, Saul is called Paul for the first time. According to this verse, where did Paul receive his power for ministry?

Read Acts 26:15–20. How did Paul respond to the call God placed on his life? What became his new message?

Turn back to Acts 9:15 and write the verse below. Circle the word(s) God used to describe Paul to Ananias, and underline what God desired to accomplish through Paul.

May we never misjudge the "instruments" or "tools" God uses to fulfill His kingdom plans and purposes. Thankfully, He doesn't require someone with a picture-perfect past. Instead, with merely mustard-seed faith, a willing heart, and a fresh filling of the Holy Spirit, God can accomplish immeasurably more than we could ever dare ask, dream, or imagine.

Apply It

We may not live in 51 AD as did the Corinthians, but we *can* very easily relate to their way of life, culture, and circumstances. What are the important things that stood out to you about the city of Corinth?

In what ways is Corinth similar to our culture today? In what ways is it different?

SIMILARITIES	DIFFERENCES

 Write a prayer for your community, asking God to send His chosen instruments to share messages of truth and grace so that all might *live full* and *walk free*.

PART TWO:
Paul's Arrival in Corinth

> **Memory Verse:** For the message of the cross is foolishness to those who are perishing, but to us who are being saved it is the power of God.
>
> —1 Corinthians 1:18

I'll never forget the first time I heard the life-changing words of the gospel. My personal life before Christ was a mess: after a childhood filled with intense hurts and rejection, I attempted to numb my pain with everything the world had to offer—food, men, alcohol, drugs, even shopping. You name it, I tried it, but nothing worked. My heart was sick with guilt and shame for the awful choices I knew I was making.

Before long, I was at the mercy of a serious drug and alcohol addiction. Every moment was motivated and driven by my addictions. I knew this was not the best life for me and my young son, but I didn't know how to stop. That is, until the dreadful day when I accidentally overdosed on cocaine and nearly died. After being rushed to the hospital, our local law enforcement agency became involved and my self-destructive ways were finally laid bare and exposed to all.

In the midst of my mess, I made a phone call to a joyful customer named Carole who frequented the restaurant where I worked. I didn't know this woman well, but I knew there was something different about her, and I wanted what she had. After listening to my troubles, Carole bravely shared four simple but transformational words—"Cindy, you need Jesus." Carole also explained from God's Word the full, free life available in Christ. Since I'd sampled pretty much everything the world offered yet still felt empty inside, I figured I didn't have anything to lose if I gave this "Jesus thing" a try.

On July 26, 1996, I invited Jesus Christ to take control of my life. Best decision ever!

If my life is a living testament to anything, it's this: God uses broken people for His beautiful purposes. How else do we explain how a former drug addict turns from "rock bottom" to restored Bible teacher? Or Paul's transformation from forceful Pharisaical fanatic to passionate follower of Christ?

Only God.

In Christ, our previous choices—the good, the bad, and even the ugly—can become the springboard to propel us forward into passionate, purpose-filled living. Thankfully God doesn't see our past; He sees our kingdom potential.

Paul knew this to be true. He understood to his core the transforming power of Jesus. Thus he became the perfect fit as God's messenger to the corrupt city of Corinth. God would use Paul to turn this warped culture upside down for Jesus' sake.

Let's join Paul as he traveled for the first time to Corinth.

 Read Acts 18:1–11. How long did Paul spend in Corinth (v. 11)?

 What would those months have been like for Paul? Imagine what he would have observed while living in immoral Corinth, and record your thoughts:

Paul would have witnessed things that distressed, frustrated, and angered him. He would have walked among the worshipers of false gods at the temples. He would have stood on the streets as vulgar parade floats passed by and heard the raucous noise of drunken

Greek dinner parties. Perhaps he would have even watched as prostitutes strolled by each night. For most Corinthians, this was mundane, everyday life.

 Flip ahead to 1 Corinthians 2:3–5. How did Paul describe his emotional state as he entered the city?

Can you blame Paul for being afraid as he entered this wicked place? Besides, before arriving in Corinth, Paul had been stoned in Lystra (Acts 14:19), stripped and whipped in Philippi (Acts 16:22–24), and barely escaped a riot in Thessalonica (Acts 17:10). Paul was terrified entering Corinth, fearing his work would be cut short by opposing Jews or the overwhelming worldliness around him. I would be shaking in my sparkly shoes for sure. How about you?

. . . our previous choices can become the springboard to propel us forward.

 Even so, what *did* Paul do while he was in Corinth (Acts 18:11)?

Paul's ministry is described simply: he faithfully taught God's Word. Paul knew a strong church in this influential city could spread the life-changing message of Jesus all over Greece and then throughout the known world.

Did you notice Paul did not arrive in Corinth with a five-step self-help strategy, a persuasive power point, or an outstanding outreach agenda? No way.

Instead, Paul went empowered by the Holy Spirit, moment by moment. The Spirit gave Paul the right words to say, whether he was talking to a wealthy merchant, a drunken sailor, or an Isthmian Games athlete. And that same Spirit can give us the perfect words when we don't know what to say to the friends, neighbors, and strangers who cross our paths every single day.

Digging Deeper

Can you imagine what it would have been like to sit under the apostle Paul's instruction? As a trained rabbinic scholar, Paul would have memorized at least most of the Torah (the first five books of the Old Testament) as well as the Prophets.[6] Wow—makes six memory verses look easy! Given Paul's fiery passion, zeal, and knowledge of the Old Testament, I'm guessing his talks would have been anything but boring and monotonous. In fact, Acts 13:42–43 tells us as Paul and Barnabas once finished teaching, the people begged them to come back the next week and speak more. A communicator's dream! (Side note: Peek at Acts 13:44 to see what happened when Paul and Barnabas returned the next week. Awesome!)

Scripture doesn't say what Paul communicated during his initial visit with the Corinthians, but we can view his correspondence with them as well as his other letters to give us an indication of his message. Wherever he went, Paul laid the same foundation: Jesus.

 Read 1 Corinthians 15:1–8. What does verse 1 tell us Paul preached to the brothers and sisters in Corinth?

In case you—like me—didn't grow up with a foundation of faith, the words *gospel* or *Good News* may sound confusing and/or "churchy." The *Wycliffe Bible Encyclopedia* describes the gospel this way:

The central truth of the gospel is that God has provided a way of salvation for men (and women) through the gift of His son to the world. He suffered as a sacrifice for sin, overcame death, and now offers a share in His triumph to all who will accept it. The gospel is good news because it is a gift of God, not something that must be earned by penance or by self-improvement.[7]

Who is offered a share in Christ's triumph? It's just a little three-letter word, but boy, is it powerful. Circle the word *all* above.

All means *you*, friend. Now draw a line through the words *penance* and *self-improvement*. Goodbye self-punishment and working hard to win God's approval! Those things are simply not required to receive the gift of God.

 Did you note how Paul succinctly summarized the essence of the gospel? Write out the key points from 1 Corinthians 15:3–4:

15:3

15:4a

15:4b

Of first importance to Paul when he arrived in Corinth was to share the life-changing, liberating message of Jesus Christ—available to *all*. Regardless of who you were, in spite of what you had done, or no matter what had been done to you—Paul knew only the power of the gospel could transform this corrupted community from darkness to light, from pleasure-seeking to purpose-filled living, from captivity to freedom.

Consider how the gospel would have radically shaken up this idol-filled culture. Paul's teachings would have been revolutionary! No longer would you have to sacrifice an animal at the temple of Apollo or bow down before Poseidon or other deities of mythology. No more would you have to participate in ritualistic, drunken behavior and sexual acts at Aphrodite's temple of love. If you were sick, you wouldn't have to ever again seek healing through clay offerings at the temple of Asclepius. To receive the free gift of life in Christ, you didn't have to *do* anything—it had already been *done* for you on the cross through Christ.

What Good News! Are you curious how Paul's message was received? Did the Corinthians toss Paul right out of town, insisting, like the Athenians, that he was a "babbler" who didn't know what he was doing?[8]

 Read Acts 18:8 below and circle the people who heard Paul, and underline how they responded.

> *Crispus, the synagogue leader, and his entire household believed in the Lord; and many who heard Paul believed and were baptized.*

May we never underestimate the power of the gospel! Skeptics must have questioned Paul's goals. "Corinth? That wicked community? They'll never change!" But Paul proclaimed anyway. "You need Jesus."

And soon he became the first pastor of a new community of Christ followers founded in Corinth.

Don't get me wrong: Paul didn't have it trouble-free. Not everyone wanted to hear his countercultural message. But by the end of his first visit in Corinth, the early church was relatively stable and secure, and Paul set sail and continued his missionary journey.

Apply It

What does the message of the cross mean to you? Check any/all of the options below:

- [ ] I'm not sure yet what the gospel means. I need to learn more.
- [ ] It's easy to go through my daily life forgetting about the cross.
- [ ] The gospel changed everything for me. I was blind, but now I see!
- [ ] Because of the gospel, I now have fresh faith and power.
- [ ] I've heard so much about the gospel over the years that sometimes I forget how transformational it is.

If you are a Christ follower, take a few moments and reflect on how Jesus has changed your life. Using the cross diagram on the next page, describe your life BC (before Christ), when/how you were introduced to Jesus, and then how your life is now different AC (after Christ). I'll go first as an example.

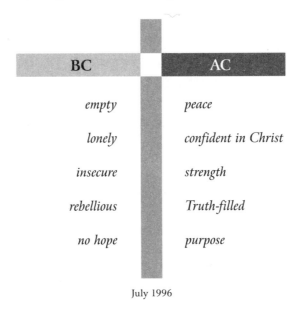

BC	AC
empty	peace
lonely	confident in Christ
insecure	strength
rebellious	Truth-filled
no hope	purpose

July 1996

Heard about Jesus from Carole and invited Him to be my Lord and Savior.

Your turn:

Whether you have been following Christ your whole life, whether you can identify with my wayward past, or whether you have just recently made this life-changing decision—your story matters! And your story could be the bridge for someone who desperately needs to hear about Jesus. May I encourage you to share this cross exercise with someone this week? Let's celebrate and share the power of the cross!

If this is your first time hearing about the Good News of Jesus, please remember, the invitation is for *all*—the sexually immoral, idolaters, adulterers, thieves, greedy, even the gossips are welcomed.[9] *No one* is too far gone; not one person has out-sinned the grace and mercy of God. (See what Good News it is!)

If you have not made this life-changing decision, would you prayerfully consider doing so now? If you would like to know beyond any doubt that you've opened the door to a relationship with Jesus Christ, I invite you to pray a simple but powerful prayer. Please know there's no magic in the words—it's not the words that save you but your faith in Jesus.

Dear God, I admit I am a sinner. I believe that Jesus Christ died on the cross for me, and that He rose again. Please come into my life. I choose to surrender to You. I invite You to take over the controls of my life. Thank You for Your great love for me. In Jesus' name. Amen.

If you prayed just now, welcome to the family of God! You have God's promise that you are His child. You are forgiven and will spend eternity with Him, and He can change you just as He has and is still changing me.

Why not sign and date this page so you will always remember this significant, life-changing day on your spiritual journey. I would also encourage you to share your decision with someone. Maybe it's the person who invited you to Bible study, another close friend, or your *Live Full, Walk Free* leader. I would love to hear from you too!

May we never underestimate the power of the gospel! The message that points to Christ on the cross seems like sheer silliness to those hell-bent on destruction, but for those on the way of salvation, it makes perfect sense![10]

PART THREE:
Know the Truth

> **Memory Verse:** For the message of the cross is foolishness to those who are perishing, but to us who are being saved it is the power of God.
>
> —1 Corinthians 1:18

Have you ever wished you could be a "fly on the wall"—an unnoticed observer of a noteworthy situation? As a mom of four kids, I often think it would be fascinating to secretly listen in and shadow my children throughout their school day. What's it really like on their bus ride? How's the conversation in the gym locker room? Is anyone unkind to them? Do they actually eat their lunch, or does it mostly end up in the garbage? Inquiring minds want to know!

Of course, I can hear my tweens telling me now, "Mom, that's creepy." I'm not saying I *do* lurk in the lunchroom or the bushes, stalking my children, but you can't blame a mom for being curious, right?

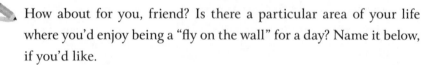 How about for you, friend? Is there a particular area of your life where you'd enjoy being a "fly on the wall" for a day? Name it below, if you'd like.

As we continue learning from Paul and his relationship with the new church of Corinth, I think it would be grand to be a "fly on the wall" in this age-old assembly of believers. What was the overall tone of Paul's messages? Did he get teary-eyed as he reflected on his Damascus Road experience? Was Paul ever funny, or was he always impassioned and serious?

What would you be curious to learn as an unnoticed observer in Corinth's early church?

As we've discovered, the Bible *does* confirm Paul spent at least eighteen months helping the rookie church in Corinth gain its footing in their slippery society. How? By building a firm foundation based on the Word of God (Acts 18:11).

Remember however, the New Testament was yet to be written. Let's not picture a bunch of believers walking through the marketplace carrying their brand-new Bibles, colored pencils, and index cards on their way to Bible study.

When Paul mentions God's Word, he is referring to the Old Testament Hebrew Scriptures in their Greek form. (To be precise, the Greek translation of the Hebrew Scriptures is called the Septuagint.) Besides, no more than 10 percent of the people in New Testament times could read,[11] so Bibles wouldn't have helped most of the population, even if they were available.

Instead, in the midst of homes all throughout the sin-soaked city, small communities gathered and listened intently as Paul shared his treasures of knowledge and insights with them. Paul wanted these new Christ followers to *know* the truth, *live* the truth, and then *share* the truth—believing a community of Christians in this popular crossroads city would not only transform their corrupt community but could impact the whole world for Christ!

Digging Deeper

In case you are thinking, "What truth are you talking about, Cindy? What *is* the truth?"—when we refer to Paul's desire for the Corinthian Christ followers to *know*, *live*, and *share* truth, we are talking about the eternal truths found in God's Holy Word. God's Word is the standard against which everything else must be tested and compared. Paul knew if the Corinthians had any hope of stability and security in their slip n' slide world, they had to gain traction on God's powerful promises.

This was deeply personal to Paul. He understood how the power of the Word works mightily inside a believer—transforming our thinking, enlarging our vision, forcing darkness out of our mind, and whooshing like a mighty force into every part of our life.

 How has knowing the truth of God's Word made a difference in your life? Is there a passage of Scripture that has been especially meaningful to you on your faith journey?

Knowing the truth is wonderful—but there is more, isn't there?

Lukewarm Christians, non-believers, and even the enemy of our souls can *know* the truth.[12] Paul wanted Christ followers to *live* the truth. As followers of Christ, our behavior, speech, attitude, and actions should reflect God's character and goodness. It's through experiencing God's Word and applying its truth to our every-day circumstances that our lives are changed and we fully experience freedom.

Although we don't know the exact spiritual principles Paul taught the new Corinthian church members, we can gain an understanding by observing his communication with other churches he founded. Let's consider the letter he wrote to the Ephesians, a church gathering located in a sinful port city directly across the Aegean Sea from Corinth.

 Look up the following verses and briefly summarize the instructions Paul communicated to the early Christ followers living in the immoral, idolatrous city of Ephesus.

Ephesians 5:1

Ephesians 5:3

Ephesians 5:11

Ephesians 5:18

Although Paul wrote these words to the Ephesians *after* his stay in Corinth, my sense is he would have given similar instructions during the eighteen months he was forming the Corinthian church. In both locations, the twisted cultures of their cities had crept into the church, to the point where little set them apart from their loose-living neighbors. Rather than modeling a new and better way to live, the early Christ followers' lives looked just like everyone else's.

Now let's be real: would it have been easy to live out these truth-filled principles in an immoral, anything-goes community? I think we'd agree—absolutely not! The peer pressure must have been unbelievable, the temptations oh so luring.

God's Word is the standard against which everything else must be tested and compared.

Everyone is tempted by different things. Let's take sex, for example. If sexual sin was your greatest, hardest-to-resist temptation, living a wholesome, disciplined life in Corinth would have been difficult. Sex and opportunities to have it were everywhere. In Corinth, "normal" included a girl generally being married at about age sixteen . . . to a man twice her age. Apart from the wedding night, it was common for married couples to sleep in separate beds, with mistresses also living in the home. Not to mention, men used female prostitutes regularly, whether at one of the countless brothels, the temple, or even at a dinner party as the "after dinner" entertainment.

Can you imagine how the mouths of the early Christians must have dropped open when Paul encouraged them to no longer live with even a "hint of sexual immorality"? Living this new way would have been a completely foreign idea! "(In Corinth) the idea that sexual immorality was wrong was like you and I saying having a cup of coffee in the morning is wrong," writes Pastor Jim Cymbala. "It was unknown. It was insane. . . . But Paul didn't care. He preached it."[13]

Heaven forbid anyone ever teaching that having a cup of coffee is wrong! I would be sunk. (And all my coffee-loving friends said "Amen!") But may we remember—*nothing* is too difficult with the power of God at work. Romans 8:26 tells us that God's Spirit helps us in our weaknesses, and Jesus promises Christians, "With God all things are possible" (Matthew 19:26; Mark 10:27). God doesn't want us to remain as we were when He called us, but instead, we're invited to experience and enjoy life, and have it in abundance—to the full, till it overflows (John 10:10 AMP). Let's pursue lives of truth.

Know the truth. *Live* the truth. But also, we must *share* the truth with others.

Personally I am super passionate about this subject. You see, no one ever shared the truth of God with me until I was twenty-six years old. No, I didn't live on an island, in a corn field, or the forest. I grew up in a conservative community with a church on nearly every corner. During my loneliest and most painful season, I worked as a pregnant, single waitress in a family-friendly restaurant frequented by Bible-carrying Christians. Nobody ever invited me to church or left a personal note scribbled on a receipt. Not a soul ever whispered in my ear "Hey, did anyone ever tell you how much God loves you?"

I'll never forget when a Christian counselor opened up God's Word and shared Jeremiah 29:11–13 with me for the very first time. I didn't even know Jeremiah was *in* the Bible. Yet the amazing *truth* that I could call upon a loving and holy God, and He would hear from *me*, infused unbelievable peace and hope into my pain-filled soul.

I couldn't help but wonder in the days to come, "God, how come no one ever told me? How come nobody ever shared your life-changing Word with me?"

May it not be said of us, "No one ever told me." Not on our watch. Truth this transformational is meant to be shared.

So back to the ol' "fly on the wall." Would unseen observers in my home, in your home, say, "Now that's a woman who *knows* the truth, *lives* the truth, and isn't afraid to *share* the truth—in love—with others"?

 ## Apply It

How are you doing at knowing, living, and sharing the truth?

On a scale from 1 to 10, with 10 being the highest, mark a "K," "L," and "S" for how well you know, live and share the truth.

Please know this exercise is not meant to bring about guilt or condemnation, and we won't ask you to share it in your small group. Let's just take an honest assessment for the purpose of a starting place, asking God to help us move forward.

After you've marked your scale, reflect on what led you to pick each number? What is one practical thing you can do this week to help your number go up one notch? Write your thoughts below.

To go from a _____ to a _____ when it comes to **knowing** the truth, I could . . .

To go from a _____ to a _____ when it comes to **living** the truth, I could . . .

To go from a _____ to a _____ when it comes to **sharing** the truth, I could . . .

Wherever you are on the scale, remember, perfection is not our goal, just progress. We've got to start somewhere, right?

Peek at the list from Part One you wrote on the inside back cover of this book. Are there passages of Scripture that can help you in these areas? Take a few moments to reflect on your list of current obstacles, and then write a prayer asking God to help you *know*, *live*, and *share* truth.

PART FOUR:
Got Issues?

> **Memory Verse:** For the message of the cross is foolishness to those who are perishing, but to us who are being saved it is the power of God.
>
> —1 Corinthians 1:18

Last month I made the dreaded visit to the doctor for my annual checkup. It's not that I don't like my physician—it's those dismal numbers I could do without. Somehow my weight keeps creeping up, while my height slowly creeps down! I'd much rather spend the afternoon pulling weeds—and I don't garden—than getting poked, prodded, and repeatedly reminded of my age and the "changes" yet to come. Good grief.

There was a spot of comedy, though, amid all those unfortunate numbers. "Do you have any issues we should be aware of, Mrs. Bultema?" the spunky nurse asked. I nearly burst out laughing. "Issues? Do I have any issues? How much time do you have?"

As I write this lesson, I have a band on my right arm to relieve my tennis elbow, a stye in my left eye, and a sore throat and raspy voice. There's a dead Christmas tree in the backyard (it's mid-March), my naughty dog Rocky drives me bonkers, and a woodpecker is making his summer home in the side of my house. And those are just the *surface* issues. If I were really honest, I've got issues to work through on the inside as well—like fear, insecurities, comparisons, and an unhealthy attachment to sparkling flavored water.

Do you have any issues you are dealing with? Take a minute and jot down a list of some of the cares and concerns you are faced with these days. (Sometimes it just helps to write them down.)

Your issues may be different than my issues, but I think it's fair to say we all have them. Whether we are young or old, wealthy or poor, sick or healthy, go to church or don't go to church, live in a condo, apartment, or our mother-in-law's basement—we all have issues.

As we've discovered, the Corinthian church members were not immune to issues, big and small. In fact, there's no way I would trade my creeping weight, stye in my eye, dead Christmas tree, and assorted insecurities for the problems faced by my brothers and sisters in first-century Corinth. Let's travel back to Corinth and take a look at some of the issues bearing down on the newly founded church. We'll be encouraged as we see how Paul tried to restore balance in this unsteady, issue-laden community of believers.

🌿 Digging Deeper

If I asked you how many letters Paul wrote to the Corinthians, chances are you probably would answer two—First and Second Corinthians.

 Before you respond, **turn to 1 Corinthians 5:9** and write out the first half of the verse below.

What letter is Paul talking about here? Let's take a moment to peek at a quick time line with approximate dates, and I'll try to clarify Paul's early Corinthian correspondence.

(Note: If the thought of a time line feels too much like schoolwork, skip right over it. I won't pop out of your kitchen closet and give you a quiz, promise.)

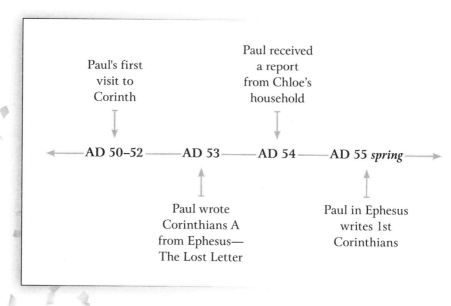

Paul's first visit to Corinth

Paul received a report from Chloe's household

◄———— AD 50–52 ———— AD 53 ———— AD 54 ———— AD 55 *spring* ————►

Paul wrote Corinthians A from Ephesus— The Lost Letter

Paul in Ephesus writes 1st Corinthians

51 AD—Paul arrived in Corinth for the first time.

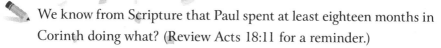 We know from Scripture that Paul spent at least eighteen months in Corinth doing what? (Review Acts 18:11 for a reminder.)

After the new church was settled, Paul continued on his missionary journey, ending up in the city of Ephesus. Using the map on the next page, put a "C" for "church" near the city of Corinth, and place a "P" for Paul near the city of Ephesus, Paul's home base for the next few years.

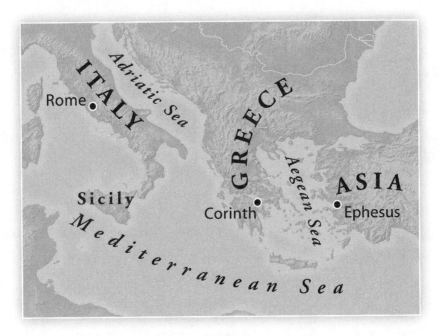

52 AD—Apollos, an "eloquent man, mighty in the Scriptures," went to Corinth to serve as the second pastor (Acts 18:24; 19:1). Add an "A" for Apollos to the map near Corinth.

53 AD— Paul wrote a letter of instruction to the Corinthians, now referred to as the "previous letter" you read about in 1 Corinthians 5:9.

Where is this "previous letter?" Nobody knows. This ancient letter no longer exists— it was lost without a trace. Scholars call it Paul's "Corinthians A" letter [14] or simply the "lost letter."

I'm glad to know I'm not the only one who loses important things.

54 AD—While Paul was still in Ephesus, a woman named Chloe sent some of her household to him to report problems within the Corinthian church. I think this is what my kids would call a "tattletale." This delegation described to Paul the disastrous state of their church.

Read the following verses to get a sampling of the issues, and write a small description of each challenge they faced.

1 Corinthians 1:10–11

1 Corinthians 3:3

1 Corinthians 5:1

1 Corinthians 6:6–7

1 Corinthians 11:21

1 Corinthians 15:12

 Which issue is most surprising to you? Explain your answer.

No doubt about it—the Corinthian church had issues! Strife and division were seriously threatening the young church. Some had become spiritually arrogant, leading to further problems such as sexual misbehavior, wrongs against other believers, abuse of spiritual gifts, and misunderstanding of basic Christian teachings. What a royal mess.

"What happened?" you might be thinking. "I thought they *knew* the truth." You're right—they did. Although the Corinthian Christ followers had been taught of the new freedom and life available in Jesus, they quickly slid back into their old sinful habits and patterns. One author shares:

> The problem with the church in Corinth was the *Christians* in Corinth. They were so enamored with the secular lifestyle that they didn't want to give it up. They lived in a culture that emphasized self-importance, ambition, and status. That's the mind-set they had before they were Christians, and they brought those same feelings into their church.[15]

Sound familiar? Underline any parts of the quote that sounds similar to our modern culture today.

Can you imagine how Paul—after having spent nearly two years pouring his life and love into this church—would have felt to receive this upsetting update? Though a few years had passed since he had been with them, Paul felt a spiritual responsibility for the young church of Corinth, and this news troubled him immensely.

About the same time, Paul also received a personal letter from some of the Corinthian church members. They had a number of specific questions they wanted to ask their founding pastor about Christian behavior, lifestyle, and doctrine. Can you blame them? Clearly, living out God's truth in their sin-flooded culture was not easy, and as first-generation Christians, they didn't have the luxury of following their parents' example.

55 AD—Paul wrote the letter we now call First Corinthians. His intent was twofold:

1. To reply to the shocking report from Chloe's household.

2. To respond to the church members' questions.

What were they asking? We can get a sense of their inquiries by reading Paul's personal response to them.

Look up the following verses to determine the various topics the church members questioned Paul about, and match them to the list of concerns on the right.

1 Corinthians 7:1–3 •   • Food sacrificed to idols

1 Corinthians 7:25 •   • Collection at church

1 Corinthians 8:1 •   • Married life

1 Corinthians 12:1 •   • Virgins/unmarried

1 Corinthians 16:1 •   • Spiritual gifts

 Which subject matter is most surprising to you? Reflect on what we've learned about the Corinthians so far. Are there any topics you are surprised *not* to see on the list?

It's not so much what the believers were asking about, but rather what they were *not* asking about. Seems kind of fishy to me that they skipped right over biggies such as inner strife, pride, incest, and sleeping with prostitutes, and they asked instead about the relief offering for the poor. Basically, they were throwing him softballs. Were they hoping Paul would not find out about their appalling behavior? One scholar thinks so, imagining the Corinthian church members having little huddles that went like this:

> We can't write to Paul about incest and sleeping with prostitutes. Besides, if we do commit such problems to writing, and send them as a letter—the letter could circulate across the church. If that happens, what would the other churches think of us? No self-respecting community hangs its dirty laundry in the front garden. No, no—we will ask him about things like divorce, remarriage and marriage to unbelievers—you know—the kinds of topics that can be discussed comfortably in public meetings.[16]

The Corinthians' sanitized list of questions reminds me of the "safe" prayer requests shared during small group gatherings. You know how it goes—stresses are high, patience is low, messes are many, and everything in you wants to run, numb out, and/or stuff the pain—but when it's your turn to share a personal prayer request, you ask for prayer for your uncle's neighbor's friend's Aunt Sue. Not that there is anything wrong about praying for Aunt Sue, but why not bring up the real issues robbing you of your peace and joy? Why not share how you are *really* doing? (Am I the only one who wrestles with this?)

The point here is this: We will never experience all God has for us until we identify the *real* issues weighing us down and tripping us up on our faith journey.

🌿 Apply It

 What issues are getting in the way of your living a full, free life? If Paul were writing a letter to *you*, what would be some of the concerns he might ask you to address on your faith journey? Circle any of the following that apply:

Debt	Legalism	Gluttony
Jealousy	Materialism	Fear
Guilt	Unforgiveness	Addiction
Self	Pride	Lies
Anger	Gossip	Comparisons
Anxiety	Worry	Critical spirit
Shame	Perfectionism	Painful past

Other:

Take time to review your list and then prayerfully journal your thoughts below.

We will never experience all God has for us until we identify the real issues weighing us down.

My prayer for you is this: May you take a risk and bring your issues to Jesus—all of them. And then may you take any suitable "next steps"—saying no to unhealthy habits, asking a girlfriend for help, or going to see a Christian counselor—so that you experience the peace-filled, abundant life that is yours in Christ. You are not alone, sweet friend. Please don't wait another day.

PART FIVE:
Special Delivery

> **Memory Verse:** For the message of the cross is foolishness to those who are perishing, but to us who are being saved it is the power of God.
>
> —1 Corinthians 1:18

Letter writing is becoming a dying art. Rather than putting pen to paper, we zip off texts, tweets, and emails—transmitting a message within mere twinkles of time. In our high-speed life and times, the youth are most affected by this change in communication. According to a poll commissioned by World Vision, four out of ten seven- to fourteen-year-olds have not received a letter in the past year, and 20 percent of children say they have *never* received a single letter in their lifetime. Plus, more than 25 percent have not written a letter in the past year, and one in ten has never written one.[17] Can you imagine?

 When was the last time you penned a letter to someone? To whom was it written?

Two thousand years ago, letters were not exactly *whoosh, zoom, whiz*. Words that might describe how long it took to first write and then send a letter are *forever, ages,* and *eons*. Talk about "snail mail"!

Thankfully Paul made it a priority to send personal letters to select individuals and churches he encountered on his gospel-sharing journeys. He wrote a whole series of letters to the confused congregation of Christ followers situated in depraved Corinth. Paul needed to address the variety of serious moral errors plaguing the spiritually struggling church—and without delay.

 Read 1 Corinthians 1:1–9, in more than one Bible translation if possible. (A second version can illuminate different aspects of the verse by using varied terms and expressions.[18]) Pay attention to Paul's tone, words, and repeated ideas as well as anything unpredicted or surprising to you. Note your findings below.

 Did you note Paul's tone? Anyone else surprised by the opening of the Corinthian correspondence? If you were in Paul's shoes, how would *you* have started your letter to this wayward church?

If I had written that letter, the tone may have been slightly different. I'm afraid the Mad Mama in me may have come out in full force. I might have given them a good old-fashioned written lecture—complete with lots of exclamation points and words in all caps. "Come on, friends, you KNOW better! It's time for YOU to shape up—or else! Don't make me come over there! I. Am. Not. Kidding!" (My kids know that when I verbally punctuate after each word, it ain't gonna be pretty.)

So Paul's manner is surprising—and revealing. In spite of his first readers' willful sins and weaknesses, Paul didn't launch into a stern scolding, questioning their fading faith. He didn't even encourage them to pack their personal belongings and hop the next boat out of town. Instead, Paul—inspired by the Holy Spirit—opened by affirming their identity and reminding them of the truth—who they are in Christ.

❧ Digging Deeper

If you've sent an email message lately, you know there is a standard four-part header including: To, From, Date, and Subject. Most letters written in the first century also followed a basic customary salutation, outlined as follows: Sender, Recipient, Greeting, and Thanksgiving. Paul included each of those elements in the opening verses of 1 Corinthians.

 Review 1 Corinthians 1:1–9 and summarize Paul's salutation.

	VERSE	PAUL'S GREETING IN 1 CORINTHIANS
Sender(s)	1:1	
Recipient(s)	1:2	
Greeting	1:3	
Thanksgiving	1:4–9	

Who does Paul list as the additional sender of this letter? Underline his name in the table.

Sosthenes who? Scholars believe he may have been Paul's secretary, who recorded this letter as Paul dictated it. He was probably the Jewish synagogue leader in Corinth (Acts 18:12–17) who had been beaten during an attack on Paul, and later became a follower of Christ. Unfortunately, we don't know for sure. (Believe it or not, Sosthenes was a popular baby name at the time—not sure it will make a comeback anytime soon.) Regardless, he was certainly known to the Corinthians, otherwise Paul would not have mentioned him by name.

 Where does Paul say the church of God is located? Circle the city's name in your table from verse 2. If you have a bright colored marker, you might want to highlight and star your circled answer for emphasis. Where is this church of God located? *Sin City!* Oh friend, sometimes God does His most powerful work in the most unlikely of places.

I mean, would we believe today that revival could ever break out in Rio? The Las Vegas Strip? The Red Light District of Amsterdam? The Corinthian experience teaches us that the light of Jesus can shine in the darkest location, and there is no place on earth too immoral for a community belonging to God to be established. Can I get a "woo hoo!"?

 Did you note the words Paul used to describe the church members in Corinth in verse 2? Record the two descriptive phrases below.

Does Paul refer to them as disappointments? Nope. Failures? No way. Hopeless mess-ups? Not even close. Clearly, the congregation *made* serious mistakes, but it didn't mean they *were* a mistake. Their issues did not define them; instead, their identity was based on their relationship with Christ. Paul started off his letter by describing them as sanctified—set apart for God—and called to be His holy people. Unbelievably, the Corinthian believers *were* holy in God's sight, regardless of their sinful living and bad behavior.

New Testament teacher Kenneth E. Bailey shares,

> The Corinthians are identified as "Those who were made holy" and who were "called out as saints [i.e., holy ones]." They were getting drunk at Holy Communion and shouting insults at each other. One of them was sleeping with (a family member) . . . . Others denied the resurrection. Yet Paul called them "saints." Remarkable! Clearly, for Paul, a "saint" meant a person who had received the Holy Spirit and not a person who had reached some undefined stratospheric level of piety. The troublesome Corinthians *were saints!*"[19]

The Corinthian church members were called to be saints in their sin-soaked city. This blows me away! I'm not sure what image comes to mind when you hear the word *saint*—but if you are picturing nuns with halos orbiting their holy heads, it may be time for a fresh perspective. The New Testament uses the word *saint* or *saints* sixty-seven times. In every instance, the reference is to *all* believers. Never is the word used of a special group of believers who serve God better than others.[20] Instead, Scripture is clear that *all* Christians are called to be saints.

🌿 *Apply It*

If you are a follower of Jesus Christ, you too have been sanctified—set apart for God and called to be holy. The truth is, in Christ, you *are* a saint! Just for fun, fill out the nametag below with "Saint" and then your first name. After writing it out, read it aloud. How does it feel to be a saint?

How might *knowing* this truth transform how you go about your daily routine?

Clearly, the congregation made serious mistakes, but it didn't mean they were a mistake.

I wish we could enjoy a warm beverage while we shared our thoughts together. How I'd love to hear your response. For sure, the call to live set apart and holy lives in our crazy, hurting world is not easy, yet thankfully we are not left to do so in our own power but in the power of the Holy Spirit. And in Christ, we have *all the power we need for all the challenges we face!*

Write someone a letter or short note this week reminding them of the truth of who they are. Pray and ask God who might need a fresh word of encouragement and write their name on the line below. Come back and put a smiley face by their name when the correspondence has actually been written, and delivered too.

_____

❧ *Video Lesson One:*
WELCOME TO SIN CITY

Use the space below to note anything that stands out to you from the video lesson. You may also choose to take notes on a separate sheet of paper.

Use the following questions as a guide for group discussion:

1. What stood out to you in today's video teaching? Any new insights?

2. Think about what you've learned about the city, people, and culture of ancient Corinth. In what ways is Corinth similar to our world today? In what ways is it different?

3. Cindy shared, "As Jesus girls, the key to living a bold life of fullness and freedom lies is seeing ourselves as God sees us." On a scale from 1 (simple) to 10 (hard), how easy is it for you to view yourself through "glasses of grace"? What would help you move up one notch?

4. The *Live Full, Walk Free* motto could be "Know the Truth. Live the Truth. Share the Truth." Of the three parts, which is easiest for you to incorporate into your everyday life? Which is the hardest? Explain.

5. Read 1 Corinthians 1:1–9 aloud. How might writing *sanctified, called, enriched,* and *blameless* on your fingers help you in the midst of your daily life this week?

CHAPTER TWO

Cliques, Fools, and Secrets

Prayer:

God, I praise You for Your powerful promises. I'm grateful You see me through Your lens of unfailing, unconditional love. Thank you, Lord, that I can know Your truth, live Your truth, and share Your powerful truth with others. Forgive me for the times when I get self-focused and forget my brothers and sisters in the faith. Please teach me how to live in peace and harmony with my church family. Shine Your searchlight on my heart, Lord, and show me ways I can increase in my capacity to love. Use me, O God, to be a bridge builder in my home, church, community, and world. In the strong, life-changing name of Jesus I pray. Amen.

PART ONE:
We Are Family

> **Memory Verse:** Do not deceive yourselves. If any of you think you are wise by the standards of this age, you should become "fools" so that you may become wise.
>
> —1 Corinthians 3:18

Bullying stinks!

I don't know about you, but when my kids are the ones being picked on, Mama feels *all* the feelings. I'm talking anger, hurt, and, in this particular case, bafflement, at who was doing the bullying and who didn't step in to stop it.

My daughter had a bit of a lisp in elementary school, and some of the boys on the school bus had made fun of her by calling her names and mimicking her lisp, of course exaggerating. Spit actually flew from their middle school mouths into my little girl's face! She came home in a puddle of humiliation.

I wanted to climb aboard the yellow bus like a mildly deranged mama bear and have a swipe or two at those hooligans, but of course, I restrained myself. (I aspire to be sanely involved with my children's conflicts.) I prayed for grace, forgiveness, and wisdom, because the main instigator was the son of a friend. Yikes!

My son was a witness to what had been happening to his sister. "Sweetie, what did you do when those mean boys were picking on your sister?" I asked.

Awkwardly, my son lowered his head and replied, "Nothing."

Heaven help me. I wanted to jump out of my skin. "Nothing? Are you kidding me? You watched your sister getting taunted and teased, and you did *nothing*? Can you help me understand?"

Before he could respond, I kept going (as moms do): "Honey, we belong to the same family—we are Bultemas. We stick together. Family members don't stand by and do *nothing* when our sister or brother needs help. Family members take care of each other."

The same is true for the family of God.

Unfortunately, the church members of Corinth had forgotten how a spiritual family operates. From tattling on each other to taking their brothers to court, the local church was a hot mess of overblown drama and bitter contention.

And Paul was extremely concerned—especially about their lack of unity.

 Read 1 Corinthians 1:10–17. Ask God to open your mind to understand the Scriptures in a fresh new way (Luke 24:45). Record any initial observations below.

Unity may seem kind of a churchy word, but as Paul said in 1 Corinthians 1:10, it just means agreeing with one another, with no divisions, no conflict. The word *division* in ancient Greek has a connotation of ripping or tearing fabric, so literally Paul begged the church members in Corinth to not be ripped apart.

 Describe the problem in the Corinthian church reported to Paul in verse 11.

The disagreements must have been heated for word to have reached Paul in Ephesus! I mean, my kids have been known to quarrel with their siblings. But if someone would have contacted me while I was in Greece to tattle on them—their disputes must have been doozies! (Thankfully this didn't happen, and my kids were on their best behavior while we were gone. Or so they say.) Fortunately, Chloe's household kept Paul in the loop, and he was fully aware of the battle raging in Corinth.

One detail brought to Paul's attention was in regard to how the saints had broken themselves into isolated cliques.

 Write out the four factions from verse 12:

I follow _____   I follow _____
I follow _____   I follow _____

When he wrote his letter, Paul knew things were super tense. The cliques had formed, and each was sure they were right and everyone else was wrong. But why exactly had these cliques developed? There are two theories:

1. In Corinth, students were encouraged to show their loyalty to their teacher by promoting and defending him publicly. This mind-set could have transferred to the Corinthian church as they openly announced which church leader they would favor and follow. It wouldn't have been the first time the culture of the city shaped the culture of the church.

2. In the large and diverse Corinthian church, the saints simply preferred different preachers.

Unfortunately, devotion to their favorite leader drove wedges between the church members in Corinth. People were disagreeing and distancing themselves from each other because of some kind of Christian celebrity popularity contest!

 Can you relate to falling into the trap of preferring the preaching or leadership style of one person over another? How have you witnessed—or experienced—this before?

Digging Deeper

I love how—in the midst of so much splitting and drama—Paul used bonding, family language to appeal to the church members.

 Write out 1 Corinthians 1:10 below.

Depending on your translation, you may have written "brother," "brothers and sisters," or maybe even "brethren." The Greek word *adelphos*, translated "brothers and sisters" in the NIV, refers to "believers, both men and women, as part of God's family."[1] *Adelphos* was one of Paul's most familiar ways of addressing Christians, using the word twenty times in 1 Corinthians alone.

Through the use of "brothers and sisters," Paul emphasized *all* Christians are part of God's family and should live together as such. From the list below, circle any/all who are part of God's family:

Hymn-singing Christians Hand-raising Christians

Gospel-singing Christians Solemn churches

Mega churches Christians with tattoos

Rural churches Christians with no tattoos

House churches Mature Christians

English-speaking churches Baby Christians

Spanish-speaking churches Young Christians

Chinese-speaking churches Old Christians

Poor churches Married Christians

Wealthy churches Divorced Christians

Loud churches Single Christians

The family of God is a beautiful thing. We may have various preferences on worship style and church size, enjoy different ways to get our praise on, and speak in a wide variety of languages and dialects—but in Christ, *we are family.*

Forgive me as I have flashbacks of my fourth-grade roller skating party—complete with my sparkly Shaun Cassidy satin jacket and bell-bottom pants, jamming to "We Are Family" by Sister Sledge. (Younger women, google it!) Great song, and even greater message.

The family of God is a beautiful thing.

We *are* family, so how in the midst of all our differences, do Christians get along? Thankfully, the Bible is filled with instructions on how to get along with "one another." In fact, there are over fifty "one another" references in the New Testament. Nearly one third of the "one another" commands address the church getting along. Take a look at a sampling below:

1. Be at peace with one another. (Mark 9:50)

2. Don't grumble among one another. (John 6:43)

3. Be of the same mind with one another. (Romans 15:5)

4. Accept one another. (Romans 15:7)

5. Don't envy one another. (Galatians 5:26)

6. Gently, patiently tolerate one another. (Ephesians 4:2)

7. Be kind, tenderhearted, and forgiving to one another. (Ephesians 4:32)

8. Seek good for one another, and don't repay evil for evil. (1 Thessalonians 5:15)

9. Don't slander or judge one another. (James 4:11)

10. Confess sins and pray for one another. (James 5:16)

Put a check by the "one another" hardest for you as you interact with your brothers and sisters in the church. Pray and ask God to empower you by His Holy Spirit to not only *know* this truth but to *live* it as well.

Can you imagine how the church in Corinth would have been different if they had lived and shared these truths with each other? Thankfully it's not too late for you and me to still make an impact in *our* church community!

Apply It

As we reflect on the Corinthian squabbles, let's ask God to help us be part of the solution, not the problem. We will never experience a full, free life in Christ if we are unable to live peacefully with our brothers and sisters.

Pray and ask God to infuse you with wisdom as you reflect on the following questions, then journal your thoughts.

 What steps can you take to prevent or correct disunity in your church?

 Can you think of any quarrels in your church or small group community that need to be addressed?

 Have you contributed to these challenges in any way?

 What might you do this week to help restore a damaged relationship with another sister in Christ?

Reread the list of "one anothers" on page 48, this time declaring them aloud as prayers. Go through the list twice, the first time praying the verses for you individually (i.e., Lord, help *me* to be at peace with one another), and the second time, praying them for your church community (i.e., Lord, help *us* to be at peace with one another).

Now that we *know* the truth, let's *live* the truth! Send a quick encouraging email or text to a sister in Christ—preferably from a different church community—with a fresh reminder that she matters to God, and she matters to you. Life delivers many reasons to be *at odds* with our sisters and brothers. Let's look for ways to be *at one* with them instead.

PART TWO:
Can We All Get Along?

> **Memory Verse:** Do not deceive yourselves. If any of you think you are wise by the standards of this age, you should become "fools" so that you may become wise.
>
> —1 Corinthians 3:18

Rodney King was an African-American resident of Los Angeles who was violently beaten when arrested by officers of the LA Police Department. The event was videotaped by a bystander, and the incident raised a public outcry among those who believed it was a racially motivated and unreasonable attack. The acquittal of the four defendants charged in the case provided the spark that led to the 1992 Los Angeles riots.[2] Many will recall Mr. King's heart-touching plea to the media during this tumultuous time when he cried out, "Can we all get along?"

Paul might have wondered the same thing when he learned of the hurtful infighting among the saints in Corinth. Having spent nearly two years pouring his life and love into planting this church, I can only imagine Paul's heartbreak to learn that these church members were ripping each other to pieces. Things had escalated to the point where desperate times called for desperate measures, and a contingency was sent across the Aegean Sea to alert Paul about what was going on.

Christians may be "saints," but we often act quite the opposite. Have you experienced damaged relationships or divisions within the body of Christ? When was the last time you wondered, "Can't we all just get along?"

Personally, my heart is most troubled when Christians criticize each other on social media. Facebook spats, Twitter feuds, and—have mercy!—vile blog comments all spiral from bad to worse. I've never seen a grudge match resolved peacefully in a 140-character tweet, have you? Instead, what happens is that Christians sling social media mud at each other, and the watching world just laughs. Worse, some latch onto our infighting as one more reason to reject our faith.

Can we all agree that the Internet is *not* the place for brothers and sisters to debate or air their disagreements?

One pastor shares, "Because of quarreling, the Father is dishonored, the Son is disgraced, His people are demoralized and discredited, and the world is turned off and confirmed in unbelief."[3] Sweet sister, may it no longer be so!

 Look up John 13:34–35. What command does Jesus give His followers? What does He say obeying this command will demonstrate?

Back to Corinth and the early church. How could a church founded firmly on the transformational teachings of Jesus get so down and dirty that Paul wondered if he would encounter "jealousy, angry tempers, slander, gossip, arrogance and disorder" on a return visit (2 Corinthians 12:20)? This sounds more like a bad reality show than an ancient church community.

Let's put our detective hats on, ask God to shine His light of truth, and see if we can't uncover some of the sources of their dissension. We've got our work cut out for us over the next few days, and we may not always like what we discover. But by getting to the root of the Corinthians' trouble, it'll help us identify if we have similar issues. Remember, to *live full* and *walk free* is our goal!

Digging Deeper

We learned earlier that the Corinthian saints formed cliques around their spiritual leaders. They put Mean Girls to shame with their snooty in-groups and exclusive circles. One faction claimed Paul as their mentor, while others named the eloquent Apollos, the apostle Peter (Cephas), or Jesus Himself (1 Corinthians 1:12). Following *their* favorite messenger became more important than living out the life-changing message. While the church members bragged about their pet personalities, they totally neglected the great priority of the church: sharing the Good News of Jesus.

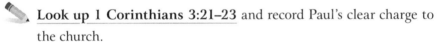 **Look up 1 Corinthians 3:21–23** and record Paul's clear charge to the church.

To discover what else the confused Corinthian Christians were boasting about, **read 1 Corinthians 1:26–31**. Make note of any initial insights and observations, then complete the chart on the next page.

(Remember, I'm using the NIV translation. If your Bible has different terms for the left column, insert them as well.)

INSTEAD OF . . .	GOD CHOSE . . . (1 CORINTHIANS 1:27–28)
The wise	
The strong	
The things that are	

Paul did not use the unflattering descriptions of the Corinthians to belittle them but to remind them they had no basis for boasting. When the Corinthians first experienced the gospel in their lives, they did not feel superior to one another nor were they divided. From God's perspective, nothing had changed between that time and the time Paul penned this letter—they still had no grounds to boast, split, or quarrel. They were brothers and sisters, and should be acting as such!

 What does this contrasting chart demonstrate about God's character, power, and heart for His children?

Scripture is filled with examples of how God shames those who seem wise and strong and promotes those who seem foolish and weak. God used trumpets to bring down the walls of Jericho. He reduced Gideon's army from thirty-two thousand to three hundred to collapse the armies of Midian (Judges 7:1–25). He used an ox goad in the hand of Shamgar to defeat the Philistines. Samson defeated a whole army with a donkey's jawbone, and Jesus fed more than five thousand people with a few loaves and fishes.[4]

Have you personally witnessed God choosing someone who appeared foolish and weak to the world for His kingdom purposes? Share an example.

The next time we feel foolish and weak ourselves (should be today if we're being real), let's remember, God chooses nobodies and transforms them into sanctified somebodies! He delights in choosing the least likely—the foolish, weak, and lowly. Why? **Review 1 Corinthians 1:29** and write it out below.

There's that word again—*boast*. You'll note as we study the Corinthian church, Paul often used the verb "to boast" when he addressed the badly behaved saints. Braggy. Pretentious. Show-off-y. These folks were guilty as charged. They had an attitude of self-confidence which seeks its glory before God and which relies upon itself—and it was damaging the church.

God chooses nobodies and transforms them into sanctified somebodies.

My takeaway? The next time we are excited to sing the praises of "our" church and its amazing programs, preaching, praise team, and coffee bar—let's be sure to give praise where praise is due. Jesus is the only One to worship.

And if we notice that complimentary comments—whether about our singing, speaking, writing, blogging, or even praying—are causing our self-importance to grow and our head to swell, let's remember: God deliberately chooses the "nobodies." (Being reminded we are "nobodies" should bring us down a notch!) May our boasting never be in what we *do* for Christ but in what Christ has *done* for us.

Corrie Ten Boom, a faith-filled Holocaust survivor, once shared, "When people come up and give me a compliment—'Corrie, that was a good talk,' or 'Corrie, you were so brave,' I take each remark as if it were a flower. At the end of each day I lift up the bouquet of flowers I have gathered throughout the day and say, 'Here you are, Lord, it is all Yours.'"[5]

Oh sister, we would be wise to do the same.

 ## Apply It

What have you boasted about during the journey of your life? Circle any/all below.

Kids	Fitness	Social media platform
Weight	Past	Cooking
Vacation	Weaknesses	Running
Grandkids	House	Diet
Spirituality	Car	Church
Job	Marriage	Bible knowledge
Testimony	Health	Sports
Gifts/talents	Prayer life	Gardening
Fashion	Friends	Photography
Man/husband	Pastor	Neatness
Grades	Hairstyle	Retirement fund
Finances	Pets	Degrees

How might boasting cause conflict in your relations with others—including both Christians and non-Christians?

The Message paraphrase of 1 Corinthians 1:30–31 says, "Everything that we have—right thinking and right living, a clean slate and a fresh start—comes from God by way of Jesus Christ. That's why we have the saying, 'If you're going to blow a horn, blow a trumpet for God.'"

 Reflect on the many blessings God has blessed you with, and spend time recording them below. Let's blow a trumpet for God!

PART THREE:
Did God Really Say?

> **Memory Verse:** Do not deceive yourselves. If any of you think you are wise by the standards of this age, you should become "fools" so that you may become wise.
>
> —1 Corinthians 3:18

Gardening is not my gift. To add insult to injury, we live in a home once known for its beautiful, picturesque landscaping. Since the Bultemas moved in—not so much. The curved brick wall surrounding our crimson maple tree collapses with shocking regularity. Unwanted weeds shoot through the cracks in our wooden deck. Once perfectly planted flower gardens are now overgrown and unkempt. It's unfortunate weeds are not in style, because our residence would be so trendy.

I may not be a gardener, but this I know: for our flower gardens to flourish once again, we must get rid of the unwanted weeds. If I'm serious about enjoying bright flowers and foliage, I need to stop whining and wishing someone else would do the work for me. It's time I put on my "big girl pants" and do the hard work necessary—get on my knees, roll up my sleeves, and pull up those nasty weeds by the root. Easy? No way. Do I want to? Not really. Worth it? Absolutely.

This week, we are asking God to help us uncover what was at the "root" of the troubles in the Corinthian church. We've learned fighting, boasting, and chronic conflict had become the norm. How did the brothers and sisters get into this mess? What can we learn from their mistakes? Together, we can dig below the surface to investigate the original source of their disagreements and difficulties.

Grab your favorite (writing) tools, and let's get on our knees and get to work, praying for the Holy Spirit to reveal truth and wisdom. We've got some persistent, pushy weeds to uproot. It's time they were exposed to the light.

 Start by reading 1 Corinthians 3:18–23, and then writing out this week's memory verse: 1 Corinthians 3:18.

Circle the word in the verse above that describes what we should become if we want to be wise from God's perspective.

I love that word *fool*. In the Greek, it's the word *mōros*.[6] Any guesses what English word we get from *mōros*?

If you said *moron*, you are correct! (I don't think I'm going to tell my kids that "moron" is in the Bible.)

As we've learned, God chooses the foolish and the "nobodies" to shame the wise and the strong. My paraphrase: "God's fools can become God's tools!" How God delights in using the weak and foolish as His chosen instruments to show the world what He is like. By choosing the morons, God alone gets all the glory when His love and light shines in our dark world.

Are you feeling foolish when faced with a gigantic God-sized task before you? Wondering why in the world you were picked for a daunting project at work? Doubting how you will ever accomplish all He is asking you to do in this season? Friend, you are in just the right spot! Be God's fool—that's the path to true wisdom, fullness, and freedom.

How were the Corinthian church members doing as God's fools? Peek at 1 Corinthians 4:10 (and yes, that's sarcasm in Paul's voice). Do you think Paul was pleased?

Since Paul spent more than eighteen months teaching the Corinthian Christ followers, shouldn't they have been actively pursuing being God's fools rather than fussing and fighting with each other? Why was there a disconnect between their *knowing* truth and actually *living* truth? What happened?

Peek back at our memory verse for a clue, and underline the first four words.

According to Webster's Dictionary, someone who is deceived has accepted "as true (or valid) what is false (or invalid)."[7] Likewise, one who deceives others convinces them to accept, as truth, something false. So, essentially we are dealing with "truth" versus "falsehoods."

> *. . . behind all deception is the "father of lies," the devil.*
> —John 8:44

As I reflect on the definition of *deceive*, I can't help but consider the elementary school "true/false" tests. Remember those? In case you've forgotten, I've created one just for you. Grab a No. 2 pencil (just kidding) and play along. It's an open-book quiz, so yes, you may use your book/Bible. In fact, I'd recommend it!

LIVE FULL WALK FREE

True or False Quiz

Directions: Read each statement aloud. Circle "T" if the statement is true and "F" if the statement is false.

In Christ . . .

1. I am accepted (Romans 15:7).	T	F
2. I am free (Galatians 5:1).	T	F
3. I am blessed (Ephesians 1:3).	T	F
4. I am forgiven (1 John 1:9).	T	F
5. I am lavishly loved (1 John 3:1).	T	F

Hopefully you have a row of "T"'s circled—the answers are all 100 percent capital "T" Truth!

Did you circle any "F"s? Or did you circle "T"s but don't really believe that the truth applies to you? If you have failed to accept as true or valid any of the statements listed above—you have been deceived. Please know, if this is the case, you are not the only one. Clearly, Paul believed Christians could be deceived, because he warned the church of deception numerous times throughout his New Testament letters. He cautioned against falling victim to deception by many things, including: sin (Galatians 6:7), self (1 Corinthians 3:18), false teachers (Romans 16:18), and even lying spirits (1 Timothy 4:1). Of course, behind all deception is the "father of lies," the devil (John 8:44). He is a deceiver, who is poised to pounce, and he would like nothing better than to catch you napping (see 1 Peter 5:8 MSG).

🌿 Digging Deeper

Let's learn from the Bible's first recorded example of deception.

Read Genesis 2:25–3:7. What question did the serpent ask Eve (3:1)?

How did Adam and Eve go from *knowing* the truth (3:2–3) to executing exactly what God had asked them *not* to do (3:6)?

Eve knew the truth. She was fully aware of God's instructions. But Satan questioned God's word ("Did God really say . . . ?"), then convinced Eve that God had told her a lie (3:4–5). The enemy used tantalizing bait, knowing Eve's heart, desires, and weaknesses. She was unsuspectingly lured, and then led astray.

Why in the world would Eve—and then Adam—listen to and believe the dishonest words of a talking serpent over the trustworthy word of God? What was Eve's response to God (3:13)?

One of the enemy's oldest tricks is sharing four simple, doubt-filled words, "Did God really say . . . ?" You see, before the devil can get his victims off course, the first thing he must do is to cause them to question God's Word.

"Did God really say . . . ?"—Maybe I didn't hear Him correctly.
"Did God really say . . . ?"—I bet if I knew the word in Greek or Hebrew, it's not what God is actually revealing.

"Did God really say ...?"—That was for their culture, but times
have changed. Why would a loving God say that?

"Did God really say . . . ?"— _____

_____

(your turn to fill in the blank)

Our culture has changed since the Garden of Eden, but God's
Word has not. Scripture is clear: the Word of God endures forever. But unfortunately for Eve, the deceitful scheme worked. She
doubted God's Word, unwisely accepted what actually was false,
and didn't take her stand on God's truth. She quickly learned an
important lesson: deception always leads to defeat and destruction.

Paul reminded the church of Eve's dreadful mistake in future Corinthian correspondence. **Turn to 2 Corinthians 11:3** and write it
here:

Where does deception begin? Circle your answer in the verse,
and then underline the result of being deceived.

Back to the "root" of the strife in the Corinthian church: deception. They were following the false messages of Corinthian culture
rather than the truth-filled way of the cross.

Instead of pursuing godly wisdom, they worshiped the worldly
wisdom of their day. They accepted the status and celebrity-driven
culture of Corinth as truth. Soon the *adelphos* were allowing the city's
culture to guide their thoughts, actions, and decisions. They deceived themselves by holding their conduct to the world's standards
and began thinking they were better off than they really were—
more knowledgeable, righteous, intelligent—and in need of nothing.

Paul pleaded with the church to turn away from worldly-wise
attitudes and to adopt God's viewpoint. God's wisdom and worldly

wisdom are greatly different and must not be confused. When we trust the wisdom of the world to guide our lives, instead of the wisdom of God, we are being deceived.

Wrong thinking leads to wrong living— every single time.

We will never *live full* and *walk free* if we embrace as our standard and norm the commonly accepted wisdom that influences our culture. We must know and think God's truth-filled thoughts on every situation. Wrong thinking leads to wrong living—*every single time*.

Apply It

The Corinthians weren't the only ones who were stuck in the mindset of their culture and needed to change their perspective. Paul said similar words to the Christians in Rome:

> *Don't copy the behavior and customs of this world, but let God transform you into a new person by changing the way you think. Then you will learn to know God's will for you, which is good and pleasing and perfect.* (Romans 12:2 NLT)

In what areas of *your* life is it easier to copy the behaviors and customs of the world than live out the truth of Scripture?

To help us identify areas where *we* may be susceptible to deception, let's compare what "the world says" versus "what the Word of God says." On the next two pages record the world's cultural messages and then note what God's Word says about the topic. (Consider the themes communicated through current TV programs, commercials, songs, and/or magazine articles.) I'll go first to get us started.

TOPIC	THE WORLD SAYS	GOD'S WORD SAYS
Beauty	*Beauty is defined by how you look on the outside. "Thin is in."*	*What matters is not your outer appearance—the styling of your hair, the jewelry you wear, the cut of your clothes—but your inner disposition.* 1 Peter 3:3 MSG
Money and possessions		1 Timothy 6:10; Hebrews 13:5
Self-worth		1 John 3:1
Forgiving others		Matthew 16:14–15; 18:21–22

TOPIC	THE WORLD SAYS	GOD'S WORD SAYS
Success/ approval		
		Galatians 1:10
Church		
		1 Corinthians 12:27; Hebrews 10:24–25
Freedom		
		John 8:32; 1 Corinthians 8:9; Galatians 5:1

The last row has intentionally been left blank for you to "make your own." Fill in a topic you sense the enemy often uses to lie to *you*—leading you to doubt God's Word and then be led astray.

 Record your thoughts on this exercise below. Close in prayer, confessing any ways you have bought into what "the world says" versus what "the Word says." Ask God to help you identify and uproot any weedy deception in your life. May He give you everything you need to follow the Word instead of following the world.

PART FOUR:
I've Got a Secret!

> **Memory Verse:** Do not deceive yourselves. If any of you think you are wise by the standards of this age, you should become "fools" so that you may become wise.
>
> —1 Corinthians 3:18

"Secrets, secrets, are no fun, unless you share with everyone."

If I had a quarter for every time I have heard this ditty, I'd head straight for the mall. As a mom of four—two girls in middle school!—our car rides often involve conversations such as:

🌸 "I'm telling Mom you're telling secrets," or

🌸 "Let me see her text. Come on—no secrets!" or

🌸 "I heard you whispering. No fair! Remember—*secrets, secrets, are no fun, unless you share with everyone.*"

Everyone loves a secret—a riddle, mystery, or surprise, something hush-hush only we are privy to. (It's just as true that we can't stand secrets when we are on the outside looking in.)

As we uncover today's lesson, we'll discover a secret Paul revealed in his Corinthian correspondence. What is the secret? What did it mean for the Corinthian church members? How can this secret help us on our journey to fullness and freedom?

Let's pray and ask God to teach us His wisdom in the secret places of our heart (Psalm 51:6), and then mine the treasures of God's Word. We don't want to miss it!

Digging Deeper

Read 1 Corinthians 2:1–16. Note any phrases Paul repeated or themes that stand out from this passage.

Depending on your Bible translation, you may or may not have noted that what Paul shared is God's secret. Read verses 6–8 from the New Century Version below, and circle the word *secret* in the text. Cross out where Paul's wisdom does *not* originate.

> *However, I speak a wisdom to those who are mature. But this wisdom is not from this world or from the rulers of this world, who are losing their power. I speak God's secret wisdom, which he has kept hidden. Before the world began, God planned this wisdom for our glory. None of the rulers of this world understood it. If they had, they would not have crucified the Lord of glory.*

The Greek word translated *secret* is the Greek word *musterion*, which signifies a "hidden thing, secret, mystery." In Paul's New Testament writings, *musterion* generally refers to things which are "outside the range of unassisted natural apprehension; and can be made known only by divine revelation."[8]

The word *musterion* makes me chuckle. We've got some *musterions* taking place at our home on a regular basis. *Musterions* such as . . .

🌸 Where do all the missing socks go? Is there a secret compartment in the dryer we are unaware of?

🌸 Who ate the last cookie or piece of blueberry bread?

🌸 How does our dog Rocky manage to reach the baked goods hidden way at the back of our kitchen counter?

Just for fun: Do you have some things in your life which are beyond human ability to determine? What secret and hidden *musterions* make up your everyday life?

As for Paul's secret, he wasn't writing about left-foot sandals missing throughout Corinth, or who nabbed the last bunch of olives at Chloe's last church potluck.

No, the *musterion* Paul was referring to in verse 7—"God's secret wisdom . . . which he has kept hidden"—was God's amazing offer of salvation for all people! Originally unknown to the prophets of prior generations, this plan became crystal clear when Jesus rose from the dead.[9] Christ's resurrection proved not only that He had power over sin and death, but He could offer this same resurrection power to His followers as well.

> *Friend, are you trying to live in your strength, or in His?*

Did you catch that? *The same resurrection power!* Can I get an "Amen"?

I love that word *power*! Paul used it in 1 Corinthians 2:4 and 2:5, as well as fifteen other times throughout 1 Corinthians. In the original Greek language, *power* is the Greek word *dunamis*, meaning "explosive strength, ability, power." It's where we get our word *dynamite*.

My favorite Greek scholar, Rick Renner, says, "[*Dunamis*] is a strength that always releases sufficient *power* and possesses the *ability* to make needed changes."[10] Dynamite power—vibrant, bold, vigorous capability! It's ours in Christ. Talk about a fantastic secret.

As Christ followers, we have access to *all the power* we need for *all the problems* we face.

All the power, for all the problems. Relationship challenges. Temptations. Exhaustion. Addictions. Mountain-sized tasks.

What freedom comes when we stop trying to accomplish everything in *our* power and mustered-up determination! Friend, are you trying to live in your strength, or in His? Let's take the pressure off ourselves and our limited abilities, and place it back on God and His limitless capabilities! He is able to accomplish far more than we could ever ask, think, dream, or imagine through His dynamic power at work in us (Ephesians 3:20)!

Question 1: I always used to wonder (maybe you did too), why would God have kept His secret for so long?

God's plan was hidden from previous generations *not* because He is an angry, unfaithful God who wanted to keep something concealed from his people. Our faithful God was waiting to reveal this Good News to everyone in His perfect timing. He is always on time, and it wasn't yet time for the secret to be revealed.

 When was the last time you recognized God's perfect timing in your life?

Question 2: Why would Paul have written of God's secret wisdom to the Corinthian Christ followers?

We've learned that Paul wrote the first portion of this letter to address the divisions and boasting in the Corinthian church. Each clique thought they possessed wisdom more superior than the others. Church members were blindly embracing the deceptive messages of their culture and seeking wisdom elsewhere. Paul hoped a fresh reminder of the glorious wisdom of the gospel would help them return to their roots of faith. He hoped the "secret" would prompt them to resume "one-anothering" once again.

✏️ Look back at your chart comparing the world and the Word on pages 65–66. In what area are you most likely to seek wisdom elsewhere? How might this impact your relationship with God? Your relationships with others?

Aren't you grateful God no longer hides His secret? We don't need to go searching for it on a TV talk show, webinar, or in a best-selling self-help book. We won't acquire it online or uncover it on Google. God gave us the Holy Spirit so we may know the amazing, mind-blowing things He has "freely given" to us.

We could never have discovered the *musterion* of God by ourselves. As 1 Corinthians 2:10 in The Message reveals, "God by his Spirit brought it all out into the open!"

You don't need a private password, an eye for detail, a sharp memory, or good logical skills to solve this *musterion*. The Holy Spirit has been provided to every believer so we can know the hidden mysteries and deep things of God.

I love how Pastor Ray C. Stedman unpacks this timeless truth:

> The deep things of God are all about how to find meaning in life, how to live an effective and satisfying life, how to be set free from guilt and shame, how to overcome bitterness and resentment, how to find love, acceptance, belonging, and forgiveness. When people realize that this secret is to be found within the walls of your church, they will break down the doors to get in.[11]

"*Secrets, secrets, are no fun, unless you share with everyone.*"

Now it's time we share God's secret with everyone. And we may have to go on a search-and-rescue mission to find the right people, because the lost are not exactly breaking down the doors to get inside our local churches. *God, help us find them so we can share your secret!*

Who might you share the secret wisdom of the gospel with this week? A coworker? Neighbor? Family member? Waitress at your favorite local restaurant?

Ask God to use you as His "tool," and then behold the astonishing opportunities He gives you. Let's join Paul in praying this: "Pray also for me, that whenever I open my mouth, words may be given me so that I will fearlessly make known the mystery (*musterion*) of the gospel" (Ephesians 6:19).

Apply It

The secret's out of the bag: The only way you and I can *live full* and *walk free* is by walking in the power of the Holy Spirit. The gospel brings the power of God into every believer's life through the person and work of Jesus and the empowering ministry of the Holy Spirit. Until the day Christ returns, we've been given God's Word as wisdom and light, and the Holy Spirit to illuminate it and guide us as we seek the truth.

Check out your obstacles list inside the back cover of your book. How might God's dynamic power strengthen you to help you overcome your challenges? How might the reminder that you hold mountain-moving power give you a fresh perspective as you walk through taxing circumstances?

Close in prayer, asking God to remind you anew of His secret wisdom.

O God, we thank You for the promise that You have given us a wisdom far greater than the world's wisdom. Forgive us for the times we have followed the ways of the world rather than the ways of Your Word. Teach us, Father, how to walk in the power of Your Spirit. Please remove anything that is getting in the way of the powerful work You desire to do in and through us. Give us the pure wisdom that comes from You as we live in our sin-soaked world. Empower us to live in unity with our sisters and brothers in Christ. Open doors so we might share Your secret wisdom with others. We want to know your truth, live Your truth, and share Your life-changing truth with others. In the powerful name of Jesus we pray. Amen.

PART FIVE:
The Temple Collective

> **Memory Verse:** Do not deceive yourselves. If any of you think you are wise by the standards of this age, you should become "fools" so that you may become wise.
>
> —1 Corinthians 3:18

In my on and off attempts to exercise and get fit, I've noticed some of the workout T-shirts my fellow gym-goers wear to encourage themselves as they melt fat and build muscle. Here are a few of my favorite slogans:

🌼 "Burpees? I thought you said Slurpees." (Ha!)

🌼 "I don't sweat, I sparkle!" (I wish!)

🌼 "Sweat is fat crying." (Except, sometimes I am the one crying.)

Naturally, Christians work out too, so there are quite a few churchy takes on the workout tee theme:

🌼 "Pray, eat, lift, repeat."

🌼 "Jesus is my Rock and that's how I roll."

🌼 "Fitness is my witness!"

Sometimes the shirts will take a Bible verse and apply it to athletic endeavors, like the muscle tank that reads: "'They will run and not grow weary,' Isaiah 40:31." I'm not exactly sure that one is quite correct, contextually, but I like the idea of not growing weary.

I do know *for sure* that the T-shirt with 1 Corinthians 3:16 imprinted on it—"Don't you know that you are God's temple"—is way, way out of context. In fact, I vote that verse may be one of the most misquoted Bible verses in all of Scripture.

 Read 1 Corinthians 3:1–17. Write out verse 16 below.

Listen to what Professor Keith Krell says about this verse:

Not only does the context support that Paul is speaking of the local church, the grammar does as well. The word "you" in this verse is plural in Greek. In English the word "you" is ambiguous—one cannot always tell if it's a singular "you" or a plural "you," for both are spelled the same. People from the South, of course, have removed that ambiguity. When they mean more than one person they say, "y'all." Well here in 3:16 Paul uses the Greek word for "y'all." Literally it reads, "Do y'all not know that y'all are a temple (singular) of God and the Spirit of God dwells within y'all."[12]

 What stands out to you from Pastor Krell's insightful observation?

Do you see why it doesn't make sense to wear this on a shirt while we're doing PiYo® or pilates? In 1 Corinthians 3:16, Paul refers to the *local church* as a temple, not to us as individuals. (In Chapter 4, we'll talk about verses that *do* refer to the individual's body as a temple, but this one does not.)

What Paul is saying here is this: "You folks *together* are like a temple—sacred, majestic, of priceless value. You *collectively* are holy and significant. God inhabits your community. So get your stuff together and start acting like it. Get along. Behave like a loving family, not a psycho dysfunctional one in some bad reality Greek tragedy."

"But Cindy," you may be thinking, "have you met my church family? Not the easiest to gel with, if you know what I mean."

Oh friend, Paul's talking here again about unity, not uniformity. Big difference. *Unity* is "being like-minded, having the same love, being one in spirit and of one mind" (Philippians 2:2). It doesn't mean all Christians will always agree on *everything,* but instead that they will agree to disagree with grace. It's harmony, sometimes very hard-earned. Unity is friendship and peace, even in the middle of differences and varied ways of looking at the same thing.

Paul's talking here again about unity, not uniformity. Big difference.

Uniformity, on the other hand, is something very different. That suggests sameness, a standardized way of looking and behaving, which could be anything from wearing matching uniforms at school to drinking the same Kool-Aid from little white cups. Paul's not asking any of us to drink the Kool-Aid. He knows we are all different ducks who quack to our own beat. But we are called to swim in the same pond without pecking each other to death!

 What does **Psalm 133:1** reveal about unity? Write the verse out below.

This reminds me of something I love in my community. Every Christmas, three very different churches take turns putting on the annual Christmas program. One church is mostly Caucasian and conservative. One is mostly Caucasian and more liberal minded. And the third is mostly African American and somewhere in the middle theologically. Yet they come together in a disarming show of unity to show how the baby born in Bethlehem is with us and for us, then and now. They put aside their own preferences on worship styles and step out of their comfy, familiar church zones and work together—collectively, communally, as one big, beautiful temple.

Digging Deeper

The problem with saints living *collectively* as a sacred temple? Saints sin.

As long as we live on Earth, we are going to experience conflict with one another, sometimes strong conflict. The early church disciples wrestled with this, disagreeing about various decisions and doctrines. Before we look at their internal disputes, let's reminisce about when the church was characterized by unity and oneness.

Read Acts 2:42–47. What was church life like for the early Christ followers?

Did this healthy community attract others to Christ? Did the church grow, stay stagnant, or struggle with members leaving the church (v. 47)?

Read Acts 4:32–35, and write out the first half of Acts 4:32 below.

Now observe how an in-house squabble impacted the early church. **Read Acts 6:1–7**. What problem had developed? How were the church members responding to it (v. 1)?

 What steps did the disciples take to solve the problem (vv. 2–6)?

Complaining, grumbling, and hard feelings within the church! *Can you imagine?!* If Christians can't get along with *each other*, how are they going to spread a message of love, hope, and unity to this lost and hurting world?

 What was the result after addressing the conflict and resolving the dispute (v. 7)?

The problem with the cliques and the conflict, the divisions and the disunity, is that they violate the very character of our loving, compassionate God. The Bible is clear: God is love, and as the church family, we should reflect His love.

Consider some of the final words Jesus shared with His disciples. The night he was betrayed, Jesus declared:

> *"A new command I give you: Love one another. As I have loved you, so you must love one another. By this everyone will know that you are my disciples, if you love one another."* (John 13:34–35)

Put a heart around all the times Jesus shared the word *love* or *loved* in the verses on page 79. Underline the clear directive Jesus shares in this passage—three times no less!

Apply It

Grace, family, love—it all sounds like sunshine and roses. But honoring God's sacred temple in the midst of our differences can be one of the hardest things we'll ever do, especially when our disagreements are deep and the stakes are high.

Let's be clear: there are legitimate times to separate from professing Christians or churches, although that subject is beyond the scope of this message. But Paul's concern for the church in 1 Corinthians 3 was *not* regarding false teachers: those spreading ideas that are not the truth of God's Word. (Paul did address this in future correspondence with the Corinthians—see 2 Corinthians 11.)

Yet Paul's message would have been instantly recognizable to Christ followers living in a temple-filled town. Perhaps he even had the limestone columns of the temple of Apollo on his mind as he penned the words:

> *You realize, don't you, that you are the temple of God, and God himself is present in you? No one will get by with vandalizing God's temple, you can be sure of that. God's temple is sacred—and you [y'all], remember, [y'all], are the temple.* (1 Corinthians 3:17 MSG)

How much importance do *you* place on the local church? Are you helping to build or blemish the church?

 On the 1 to 10 scale below, with 10 being the highest, draw a stick figure to represent how much significance you place on building your local, sacred "temple."

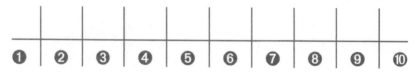

What is one practical thing you can do this week to help your number go up one notch?

Read through the following list of examples. Draw a line through the entire statement if it describes how one might vandalize God's temple, and circle ways to esteem God's sacred temple. I'll get us started.

1. ~~Ignore a blatant sin issue in the church.~~

2. Pray for your church leaders.

3. Spread discord about the women's director's new Bible study selection.

4. Forgive the church member who hurt you.

5. Criticize the new song selection from the worship leader.

6. Set up a meeting with a church staff member to address a specific concern.

7. Speak the truth in love to a small group member.

8. Critique your pastor's sermon over coffee during your Sunday school class.

9. Dress modestly so that men and women can focus on worship, not your body.

10. Share someone else's "prayer request" as a way to tell their deep, dark secret, when you know it is really gossip.

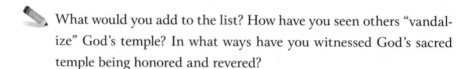

What would you add to the list? How have you seen others "vandal-ize" God's temple? In what ways have you witnessed God's sacred temple being honored and revered?

Write a prayer for your local church, asking God to help your brothers and sisters display God's oneness and unity. If you've not found a church community to call home, ask God to direct your steps and lead you to a Bible-teaching, Jesus-loving church home. May God help us all to agree with each other, love each other, and be deep-spirited friends.[13]

Video Lesson Two:
CLIQUES, FOOLS, & SECRETS

Use the space below to note anything that stands out to you from the video lesson. You may also choose to take notes on a separate sheet of paper.

Use the following questions as a guide for group discussion:

1. What stood out to you in today's video teaching? Any new insights?

2. This week we studied the first problem Paul discussed with the Corinthian church members—divisions in the church. Why is Christian unity a witness to the world? How does Paul's message of unity and oneness apply to us as Christ followers today?

3. Look up the following verses: Psalm 133:1; John 17:11, 23; and Ephesians 4:4–6. How might we live out these truths in the midst of our everyday, ordinary lives?

4. "We are on the same team." Of the three application points Cindy shared regarding what *not* to do as teammates, which is most helpful for you to remember? Which is the most difficult to live out?

5. Have a volunteer read aloud 1 Corinthians 3:18. How has this Scripture memory verse been impacting you? What Scripture memory tips can you share?

CHAPTER THREE

New Hearts, Old Habits

Prayer:

Heavenly Father, I love You. Thank You for setting me apart in my sin-soaked world, and for filling me with Your mighty, *dunamis* power. I am so thankful that You give me new hope, joy, strength, and purpose. I acknowledge You as King of Kings and Lord of Lords. Forgive me for the times I forget You are God and I am not. I confess it is easy for me to judge, critique, and compare myself to others. I am so sorry. Teach me how to best relate with others so that I can shine Your light and love everywhere I go. In the mighty, holy name of Jesus I pray. Amen.

ve Full Walk Free*

PART ONE:
Judge Not?

> **Memory Verse:** You were washed, you were sanctified, you were justified in the name of the Lord Jesus Christ and by the Spirit of our God.
>
> —1 Corinthians 6:11b

A few years ago, my marriage hit a painful pothole in the road (and by "pothole" I mean one of those swallow-a-VW-Bug craters). I loved John, but for a while there I didn't know if my marriage would make it.

I wrote some bare-my-soul blog posts. I cautiously told my readers about our painful season of marriage. "Be warned," I wrote. "If you see me at Starbucks, I may come unglued."

Thank God, my marriage made it, with help from Christian friends, a counselor, and mentors. I was bruised and dented, but I—*we*—were out of the hole—and on the healing path.

Then one day I got a phone call from a Judge-y Judy.

She was the coordinator for an upcoming event I was to speak at, and she and the committee had read my blog. They had some "concerns," and I was the subject of an "emergency meeting." *Gulp.*

(They say don't shoot the messenger, but what happens if the messenger shoots you?)

"Judy" *didn't* say "Is everything okay? We want to check in on you—how can we pray? Anything we can do to help?"

Nope. Instead, she pummeled me.

"We strongly question whether you can still teach God's Word."

"We have concerns about your faith and we doubt your focus is in the right place."

6

And, the *piece de resistance*:

"We are wondering if you should just stay home and work on being a better wife and mother."

I tried to be gracious, hanging up the phone with the air sucked out of my lungs. I could hardly believe my ears. After a season of clinging to my faith and making God-honoring choices for my marriage, this judgment was the last thing I needed.

Have you ever felt judged, criticized, condemned by your sisters or brothers in the church?

I've heard countless stories, so my guess is, you may have too.

Please know I am so, so sorry. That's not how Christ intended the church to operate. We get out our measuring sticks and evaluate, critique, judge. And, unfortunately, "Judy" is far from the first church lady to whack someone with that thing.

Take the church members in Corinth, for example. We know they were a judge-y, pride-puffed group. Their attitudes mimicked their culture, which prized certain "celebrities" and looked down their noses at whoever didn't follow the same ones. It was like the church was hosting a pastoral popularity contest, with different members being incredibly critical of the leaders based on their teaching style.

Everyone thought their group was #awesome. If they had had Twitter back then, their tweets might have looked like this:

❀ "Loving that last sermon by #Cephas. As a Jew, he can preach the other "leaders" under the table, IMHO. #TeamCephas #KnowshisOT

❀ "As for me and my house, we follow #Apollos. A mind is a precious thing to waste, amirite? #brainpower #Greeksrsmarter

❧ "Just a #humblebrag shout out to #PastorPaul. We just happen to think he knows what he's talking about, unlike some other people around here." #Romansrright

Now, there's nothing wrong with admiring a certain pastor or leader, but the Corinthian cliques were tearing the church apart with jealously and one-upmanship. Not to mention *STUCK-upmanship*. They had a major problem with arrogance, and their haughty attitudes about which leader was best had no place in the temple of God.

Pride has been called the mother of all sins, or the root of all evil—take your pick. Paul knew he had to address this bad, bad root and help his church members yank it out. They were much too influenced by the world, and had forgotten that because they had brand-new hearts in Christ, they were *supposed* to live radically different. Paul needed to deal with their wrongheaded ideas about genuine Christian leadership.

❧ Digging Deeper

Read 1 Corinthians 4:1–13, Paul's continuing plea for unity amid the Corinthian conflicts. Did Paul care if he was judged by anyone? Why or why not (vv. 3–4)?

What were the Corinthian believers to judge in regard to their leaders'—or their own—service to God (v. 5)?

Judge nothing? Are you sure?! How can that be? Everyone judges sometimes, right? Remember Judge-y Judy and her awkward phone call? Pronouncing judgment on others seems like human nature. Thankfully, Paul provided some clarity in verse 6.

Read 1 Corinthians 4:6 below, and circle the two words Paul used to describe what Christ followers will *not* be if they learned from Paul and his teaching. [Hint: rhymes with stuffed pup.]

> *Then you will not be puffed up in being a follower of one of us [minister or teacher] over against the other.*—1 Corinthians 4:6

Paul said if we leave the judging to God, we won't be "puffed up," or literally "inflated with pride." No kidding, *puffed up* is a Greek word meaning "to inflate, blow up, to cause to swell up; be proud."[1] It's derived from the same Greek word for *bellows*, which was used to blow on a fire to supply it with air.

Not by accident, Paul used this Greek word six times in his letters to the Corinthians but only once in all

The Corinthian cliques were tearing the church apart with jealously and one-upmanship. Not to mention STUCK-upmanship.

his other writings! Obviously, he thought it bore repeating with this big-headed crowd. Yes, the ancients in the assembly were full of hot air when it came to their own self-importance and pride—and it was doing harm to the work of Jesus.

The worst part: they based their judgments on outward appearances, a very unwise thing to do. (Didn't their moms ever tell them not to judge a book by its cover?) The egotistical Corinthians actually assumed they were knowledgeable enough to judge in God's place. Rather than using truth-filled standards as their measuring stick, such as:

❀ Is this person sharing truth?

❀ Does this message promote Jesus?

❀ Is the power of God resting on this leader?

- Is there fruit, or God-honoring results, in their life and ministry?

. . . this church filled with puffy stick-whackers arrogantly used worldly wisdom to evaluate the leaders and their message, such as: the style, the subtleties of the sermon, the manner of speaking. They judged the way the messenger delivered the message rather than the content of the message itself.

We would never do that, right, friend?

Or are you guilty—like me—of occasionally holding up a puffy evaluation stick to the pastors, Bible teachers, and/or leaders in your life?

Perhaps it was on your car ride home after church? Or maybe around the Sunday dinner table?

"Did you like what he said this morning? What'd you think of his sermon?"

"No, the message was too long. I've heard that verse taught better before. He drives me crazy when he paces like that. Not really enough sticky statements to help me remember it."

Or maybe while watching a teaching series online? You found yourself checking out the Bible teacher's hair, makeup, or outfit selection? You weren't even listening to the message, just evaluating the messenger's personality and personal style.

True confession time: Are you ever a Judge-y Judy? When was the last time you picked up *your* measuring stick to evaluate, critique, or judge? Looking back, how might you have responded differently?

Let's stop being puffy. We will never experience Christ's fullness and freedom if we are inflated with pride and self-importance. Paul said when it comes to relating to our leaders and teachers in the church, "*judge nothing* before the appointed time." Basically, leave the measuring stick to the only One who can use it with perfect fairness and mercy.

 Instead, how should Christ followers view their pastors and leaders? **Peek back at 1 Corinthians 4:1** and circle the two correct answers below.

Chiefs	Nobodies
Stewards/entrusted ones	Bestsellers
Rock stars	Celebrities
Minions	Popular ones
Servants	Big shots
American Idols	Bosses

Fascinatingly, the word Paul used for *servants* is the Greek word *huperetes*. Everyone who read Paul's letter would have instantly known what *huperetes* meant. Corinth was a major port city where war galleys—large seagoing vessels—often docked. The brothers and sisters in the church knew this type of boat well; they knew it had three levels, and that the under rowers (*huperetes*) sat on benches in the lowest level, powering the ship.[2]

When my husband John and I were in Greece, we learned about the under rowers and the significance of Paul using that specific term. We had taken a twenty-minute boat ride on the crystal-blue Aegean Sea to an island around which the historic Battle of Salamis had taken place. Being there, near the sea, smelling the fishy smells and tasting the salt in the air, reinforced how central everything maritime was to the people.

It was in this nautical locale I first understood how vital Paul's use of "under rower" was to his message. Or, more to the point, how vital the relationship between the under rowers and the captain was. Professor Gordon Franz, a gifted Biblical archaeologist who taught us on our trip, shared:

> The crew of the *HMS Corinth* was mutinying to the will of the captain of the ship and admiral of the fleet, Admiral Jesus, by following different personalities on the ship and not the captain. At the stern [back] of the ship, above deck, was the captain with a young man who beat the cadence of a drum. The captain would say "Stroke!" The drummer would beat the drum "Boom!" The rowers would stroke their oars in unison. Again: "Stroke," "Boom," and another united stroke of the oars by the rowers. If all the under rowers were "rowing to the beat of different drummers," the ship would be stranded in the water and go nowhere.[3]

Can you imagine how chaotic a boat ride would be if the rowers weren't following the same drumbeat? Paul wanted his letter recipients to listen to the Captain, and stop making everyone seasick with their confusion, infighting, and bragging. In essence he was saying, "Hey, don't make me, or Peter, or Apollo your captain, because there's only One of those. Instead, think of us three leaders as under rowers, volunteer citizens, working together to exalt and obey the one true Captain."

❧ *Apply It*

Nothing can twist Jesus' message more than human pride and desire for popularity. How the enemy would love to keep us divided and full of dissent rather than paddling in sync and perfect unity. It's time to be kingdom coworkers, not competitors.

What should we do when we're tempted to get puffy and judge-y with our fellow siblings in Christ? May we remember, and declare, the potent word *STOP*.

Pretend you're at church on a Sunday morning, and rather than focusing on worshiping God, you're worried if the beautiful guitar player is singing in tune. Or whether her shirt was the right choice for church? (Am I the only one?)

Here's what we can do instead: STOP.

S—Share your struggle with God. Acknowledge your wrongdoing, and confess your sin to God. "God, I am sorry. I shouldn't be judging my sister. The root of my judgment is pride, and I don't want any pride in my life. I am focusing more on her than I am on You. Please forgive me for (fill in the blank)."

T—Thank God for your brother or sister. "Thank You, God, for the gifts you've given to her and that she is willing to use her abilities for Your kingdom purposes. Thank You that we are on the same team."

O—Observe God-given qualities in your brother or sister. If you're having a hard time not critiquing, focus on positive qualities instead. "Wow, what a beautiful heart she has! What kindness she displays, and what a joyful servant she is."

P—Put down your measuring stick, and put on your glasses of grace. "God, I need to let You be the judge. That's not my job. May I stop judging, stop being puffy, and see my beautiful sister through glasses of Your grace, with a lens of Your unfailing love."

 Is there a fellow brother or sister you are pretty practiced at judging? Join me in prayerfully putting down your measuring stick, inserting his/her name in the blanks below.

Dear God, I am sorry. I confess I have judged _____ for _____ . The root of my judgment is pride, and I don't want any pride in my life. Please forgive me. I thank You for _____ and for the grace You've given him/her in Christ Jesus. May I extend the same grace to _____ which You have generously extended to me. Help me to observe _____'s gifts and talents. Help me to put down my puffy measuring stick and permanently put on Your glasses of grace. In Jesus' name. Amen.

PART TWO:
Scandal in the Church

Memory Verse: You were washed, you were sanctified, you were justified in the name of the Lord Jesus Christ and by the Spirit of our God.

—1 Corinthians 6:11b

Let's call him Wayne, although that's not his real name. Wayne was one of those guys you would look at and think—that guy has his act together. He was top of his class in college and had risen steadily in whatever company he worked for. With a lovely wife and three attractive children, Wayne seemed to be living the epitome of the American dream.

But Wayne wasn't happy. His relationship with his wife was unraveling, except he didn't know how to fix it. He was embarrassed to tell anyone, especially not anyone at his church. What would people think of him? He taught an adult Sunday school class, making some use of his Bible college education. Wayne's reputation meant something to him; so even though he had started to peek at porn, he kept up the facade that he was a great Christian guy, a happy husband, and devoted father.

Until one day, he wasn't. The occasional porn turned into a longing for a flesh-and-blood woman. Wayne created a dating site profile and started flirting with women online, and then he began to hook up with some of them on his business trips. He quit teaching his Sunday school class, citing busyness and travel, and no one questioned it. Then one of his daughter's friends from church came over and spotted something "inappropriate" on Wayne's computer. She told her parents, but they decided it was none of their business.

One day, guilt over cheating on his wife seized him, and Wayne told a neighbor friend, Max, about his fooling around. Max, a self-described agnostic, was appalled. How could Wayne, a church-goer, cheat on his wonderful wife, Max's wife's dear friend?

But his neighbor's negative response did little to stop Wayne in his lustful pursuits. Soon, he was looking at more explicit porn. When he began to wonder if he had a problem—a sex addiction—Wayne finally broke down and told his buddy Gregg, who was on the deacon board of his church.

"Oh, geesh, Wayne, it's not that big of a deal," Gregg said, patting him on the back. "All guys look at naked girls from time to time. You'll get no judgment from me!"

Gregg might have been gracious, but he also had a big mouth. News about Wayne spread like a forest fire. Half the guys who heard were as shocked as Max was but decided not to say anything. Who were they to tell Wayne how to live his life? They had each harbored lustful thoughts of their own plenty of times. The other half acted concerned when they heard the news, but really, they were secretly not surprised. Isn't this every man's battle? And if Wayne, their former Sunday school teacher, was living this way, perhaps it wasn't that bad after all. Maybe they wouldn't be so prudish next time they were traveling and surfing the TV options in their hotel rooms.

Meanwhile, Max, the agnostic neighbor, was ticked. Weren't Christians supposed to walk the line when it came to "family values"? Max didn't get it. When a local church plant dropped off a flier about their new outreach gathering, Max quickly slid it through his shredder. "There's no way I'm having anything to do with church or church people," he said. "No way!"

What would you do if you were Wayne's wife and you found out about his struggle? Or if you were one of Wayne's friends?

Although Wayne's story is fictitious, it's sadly a common one I hear all too often from women in churches all over the country. What's the "right" response? Should brothers and sisters take action when there is unashamed sin in the church? Does it matter what the sin is?

A scandalous tale—not unlike Wayne's—played out two millennia ago in Corinth. News reached Paul that his beloved Corinthians, with their new hearts, were behaving in old, disgraceful ways. Although the Corinthians *knew* the truth, they were having a hard time *living* the truth. Their lives didn't look much different than their corrupt culture.

Paul couldn't stand by and do nothing. He composed specific words to share with church members who were not addressing obvious immorality in the church. Though it's not our role to conceitedly judge the *huperetes*, we do have a responsibility to deal with sin in the lives of our church family. Let's learn from Paul's candid comeback to the horrible state of affairs taking place *in the church*.

Digging Deeper

Get a load of this unpleasant report: **read 1 Corinthians 5:1–13**.

 What was the problem described to Paul (v. 1)?

 What was the response of the Corinthian Christ followers (vv. 2, 6)?

Paul was shocked by the sin. A guy in the church was hooking up with his *stepmother*—ewwwww! Even in perverted, prostitution-happy Corinth, this was going too far. The pagans considered this to be incest! As shocked as he was by the sin itself, Paul was even more horrified by the church members' failure to take it seriously. They didn't deal with their brother's repugnant behavior, and moreover, they were proud of it. Apparently, they had actually been boasting about how tolerant they were toward him!

Sound familiar? Our culture *loooooves* to be tolerant—relaxed, open-minded—you know the drill. "Who am I to judge?" is definitely one of our favorite mottoes. Actually, it's become our default attitude.

"Oh, Amy is chatting with her ex-boyfriend on Facebook? Well, that doesn't sound very smart, but I'm not going to throw a stone."

"Brad's wife caught him looking at porn? I should say something, but then again, it's none of my business, is it?"

"Carrie's been hitting the Margaritas a little too hard this summer? I'm not going to be one of those uptight, judge-y church ladies about it."

A maybe-affair, a possible porn problem, a few nights of drunkenness—these may not seem as drastic as Wayne's story, or the story of the Corinthian church member—let's call him Julius—who was sleeping with his stepmother. But the truth tells us that every sin, even "smallies," can lead to bigger sins with whopping consequences. The struggle is real—uncorrected sin confuses and divides the church, and it blemishes the beauty of God's sacred temple.

The Corinthians may have been blind to the devastation that this immorality threatened to bring upon their friend *and* the church, but Paul knew this sin needed to be addressed, and quickly. One Bible commentary says:

> Paul was writing to those who wanted to ignore this church problem. They didn't realize that allowing public sin to exist in the

church affects all its members. Paul does not expect anyone to be sinless—all believers struggle with sin daily. Instead, he is speaking against those who deliberately sin, feel no guilt, and refuse to repent. This kind of sin cannot be tolerated in the church because it affects others. We have a responsibility to other believers.[4]

In Wayne's story, we can see how the sin spread like an evil little bacterium, first in his life, and then in the lives of others. Fellow Christians turned a blind eye, and then their own morals began to loosen. The "pagan" in his life, his agnostic neighbor Max, was repulsed by Wayne's actions. Wayne's slide into deeper sin had a corrupting influence on his church friends, and a corrosive influence on Max. This is how sin operates—it always spreads and contaminates.

 Paul selected an interesting visual to help the Christ followers see the flagrant sin issue and its impact in their community. **Peek back at 1 Corinthians 5:6–8**, and fill in the blanks from verse 7 below:

"Get rid of the _____ _____ *that you may be a*
_____ _____ _____ *—as you*
really are." —1 Corinthians 5:7

Paul used the analogy of yeast, "leaven," and rising bread dough, a metaphor that would have hit home with the Corinthians. The saints in Sin City would have known that this was a reference to Passover, or the feast of unleavened bread (Exodus 12:15). The Jews in Corinth would have celebrated this feast every year, as they do to this day. Matzo ball soup, anyone? Yum.

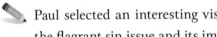 In the Scriptures, yeast is often a symbol of sin. Rewrite verse 7 below, substituting the word *sin* for *yeast*.

Does this analogy help Paul's command make more sense, especially to those of us who happen to like soft, fluffy loaves of bread?

Although as Christ followers, the Corinthians may or may not have picked up on all the ties of unleavened bread to the Jewish Passover, they would have understood that for the sake of the purity of the body, the old yeast of immorality had to be removed. And just as a pinch of yeast makes a whole loaf rise, in the same way, just a tiny bit of rotting, sour sin can permeate and corrupt the entire church. Public sin like Wayne's and Julius' affects everybody, and we as believers need to deal with it *before* it spreads.

"Hey, quit it," Paul was saying. "Quit allowing guys like Julius (and Wayne) to carry on with their immoral choices, and for the love of all—quit bragging about how accepting you are! Allowing these sins to continue has a bad effect on everyone. Your boasting is confusing and divisive; you guys need to start acting like the pure and wholesome community of believers God has called you to be."

> *Part of "one anothering" is having the courage to "pull up a chair" and share.*

Apply It

Let's be real: there is nothing comfortable about applying this passage of Scripture. Gracefully calling out sin in the lives of a brother or sister in Christ is not my idea of a fun time. No one wants to be misinterpreted, unfriended, or labeled "a hater." It'd be much easier to "simply look the other way and hope it goes away on its own, rather than bring it out in the open and deal with it in the authority of Jesus our Master."[5]

Yet Paul's instructions are clear: as family members, we have a responsibility to our brothers and sisters, to our fellow saints. We are not free to turn a blind eye when other believers have stumbled far off the narrow path. Part of "one anothering" is having the courage to "pull up a chair" and share—with grace and truth—when our community members are not *living full* and *walking free*.

Paul communicated a similar message to the church in Galatia. **Look up Galatians 6:1** and write it below.

When was the last time you were notified of a blatant sin issue in your small group, Sunday school class, or church community? How did it make you feel? Circle any/all words that apply.

Grieved	Confused	Sad
Tolerant	Forgiving	Anguished
Surprised	Disgusted	Narrow-minded
Judgmental	Open-minded	Grace-filled
Horrified	Loving	Other:

How did you respond? Looking back, do you wish you would have said or done anything differently?

In tomorrow's lesson, we'll discuss more *practically* how we might go about having these conversations. I don't have all the answers, but I've tried—and failed—at some attempts to help restore a wayward sister.

But before we think about others in our community who are struggling with sin, let's examine our own hearts and minds. Second Corinthians 7:1 in the Amplified Bible reminds us:

> *Therefore, since we have these [great and wonderful] promises, beloved, let us cleanse ourselves from everything that contaminates body and spirit, completing holiness [living a consecrated life—a life set apart for God's purpose] in the fear of God.*

 Is there any "yeast" in your life that is defiling or distracting you? Are there any old habits impacting your ability to *live full* and *walk free*?

Spend time in prayer. Use Psalm 19:13–14 from The Message as a starting place:

> *Clean the slate, God, so we can start the day fresh! Keep me from stupid sins, from thinking I can take over your work; then I can start this day sun-washed, scrubbed clean of the grime of sin.*

Acknowledge any and all *unconfessed* sins—past, present, and future! Close in prayer by thanking God for Jesus, your Passover Lamb, and for making you a new batch of dough free of any sinful yeast.

PART THREE:
Sticky Stuff

> **Memory Verse:** You were washed, you were sanctified, you were justified in the name of the Lord Jesus Christ and by the Spirit of our God.
>
> —1 Corinthians 6:11b

One thing I love about Paul's message to the Corinthians is how it teaches us to deal with "sticky situations" in life, such as:

🌸 What do I do when I don't agree with a fellow church member on a controversial doctrinal issue?

🌸 How should I respond when there's so much immorality everywhere I look?

🌸 Is it okay to say something to a sister who is making terrible choices in her personal life?

That last question? Really sticky stuff—I'm talking gum in your child's hair sticky. Or gluing your fingers together with super glue sticky. It's no wonder we'd rather avoid confrontation of this sort.

Yet according to Paul, the truth teaches us that correcting those we love—our *adelphos*, or brothers and sisters in Christ—is vital to the health and beauty of the collective temple. It's not an option to avoid these sticky messes, not even in our society which values tolerance above almost anything.

As we've read, Paul braved an excruciatingly sticky situation: a church member was openly sleeping with his stepmom, and worse, the saints were being supremely open-minded about his sin. They were even bragging about how laid back they were. *Hey, don't be a hater,* they seemed to be saying. *We won't judge you. We're free, you know!*

That two-thousand-year-old situation called for *intolerance*, as do some sticky situations we face now. Sin affects everybody, and it's our responsibility to *not* just stand there and do nothing.

It's important that we put down our pride-filled measuring sticks and not be a "Judge-y Judy." It's also imperative to "pull up a chair" and listen with compassion and kindness. Paul shares an additional approach with the church in Ephesus—and us.

 Turn to Ephesians 4:15 and summarize Paul's strategy below.

Is speaking the truth in love to a sister in Christ always enjoyable, convenient, or comfortable? Um, no. Trust me on this one. But is it necessary? Absolutely. Letting a much-loved friend walk deeper and deeper into sin is like letting her walk further and further into a flamed-filled house which is ready to explode.

In fact, Jude—brother of Jesus and James—provided an interesting word picture with regard to helping a brother or sister caught in sin.

 Turn to Jude 1:23 and write it below.

Did you note what action Jude said we must take when we find a sister/brother who is caught up in sin? He said we must act quickly to "snatch them out of the fire." The word *snatch* comes from a Greek word for pulling someone out of a dangerous situation, or to seize.[6]

Jude uses the word *harpazo* to tell you that sometimes people are so deceived about what they are doing, they don't want to change.

Even if you tell them that they are headed for trouble, they may not believe it! In those cases, your sweet words and tender pleading with them may not work . . . . Instead, your words must reach out and seize their hearts.[7]

 How might Jude's words persuade you toward action the next time a sister or brother indulges in sin? Is there anyone you know right now who is in danger of being consumed in a "fire" of sinful choices?

Have you ever noticed sometimes God will direct us to head into a "fire," even if we too might get burned? Are we willing to take that risk? The cost can be high, as I know all too well.

Several years ago, one of my closest friends was going through a tough time in her marriage. "Jenna" was precious to me; in fact, she had faithfully stood by my side as John and I transitioned through some challenging seasons together. She was my "it's okay to call at 4 a.m." friend. I loved her as if she was my flesh-and-blood sister. We were bonded.

Jenna's husband was not winning any Husband of the Year awards. He was checked out, emotionally unavailable, and refused to go to counseling with her. One day, she told me she felt God had given her permission to "be released" from her marriage. Immediately I felt she had stumbled on the wrong path. Why would God give her permission to do something—get a divorce—that He says in His word He detests? So I pulled up a chair and tried to speak the truth in love.[8]

"I love you, Jenna," I said. "I believe your marriage is incredibly hard right now, but I also don't sense divorce is God's best for you. I'm willing to do whatever I can to help you. May I encourage you to not give up?"

In my heart, I felt I had done the right thing and had tried to wrap my support in grace. But Jenna felt judged. She wrote me off that day, and every day that followed. For months, I heard nothing from her, until one day I was sideswiped by the new reality of our friendship. She had a birthday party, and I found out about it afterward. When I asked a mutual friend why I was not on the guest list, the friend looked pained. "Jenna asked specifically that you not be invited," she said.

Ugh. It was horrible. "Why didn't she say something to me? Why did she just go behind my back and make sure I wasn't invited to her party?" I blubbered to another friend. I didn't think I could live without my dear friend in my life, but I was forced to. She just couldn't forgive my attempt to speak the truth in love.

I'll be honest—this Ugh Episode in my life has made me a bit gun-shy about speaking the truth in love. Now any time a situation comes up where I feel prompted to speak to a friend in trouble, I feel a tinge of fear. "Will this friendship end up like mine and Jenna's?" I wonder.

Digging Deeper

Let's look at another example—this time from God's Word. The prophet Nathan may have wondered if his friendship with King David would survive a much-needed confrontation.

 Turn to 2 Samuel, and write out the first sentence of 2 Samuel 12:1 below.

The Lord didn't just send a prophet to confront David, He sent a friend. David had lusted after another man's wife—Bathsheba—and then had that man killed to cover up his sin. Coveting another man's wife, adultery, murder—the shepherd king had broken three of the Ten Commandments.

Now, Nathan could have been intimidated by David—he was a king, after all! David had Uriah, Bathsheba's husband, murdered—what was to stop him from murdering Nathan, too? Nathan also could have defended his friend. He could have attempted to justify David's sins. But Nathan obeyed God and confronted David. How he did it was the interesting part.

 Read 2 Samuel 12:1–14. Note what stands out to you regarding sharing the truth in love, and record your insights below.

Nathan truly "pulled up a chair." It was his knowledge of his friend that equipped him to confront David with great wisdom. God used the loving rebuke of his friend to open David's eyes.

 How did David respond to Nathan? (See 2 Samuel 12:13)

Rather than respond with bitterness toward Nathan, David saw the love of a friend. He understood what courage it must have taken for Nathan to confront him.

Let's take a page from Nathan's book. Nathan carefully, prayerfully, thoughtfully spoke the truth in love. He was willing to risk it all to save the king—to save his friend. That's friendship! The gloomiest hours of life reveal the greatest friendships.

Apply It

Imagine what could happen in the lives of our friends, family members, and churches if we really loved one another enough to go into a "burning house" and seized our sisters and brothers in Christ! Or if we courageously signaled to a friend at the first sign of smoke or a red-hot front door? How different things might be if we didn't stand by and do *nothing*?

If you—like the prophet Nathan—sense God is calling you to address poor choices in a sister or brother's personal life that you perceive as unashamed sin, I recommend that you take the following five steps.

You may want to use the fingers on your hand to help you remember.

Step #1:

Don't say anything until you've first made it a matter of personal prayer.

[Thumb: (*pointing to me*) Help *me*, God.]

Spend time getting your heart right before God. Ask God to make you a clean "tool" (Psalm 51:2) and to examine your motives (Psalm 139:23). Prayer puts you in a position where God can speak to your own heart, and He can open your eyes, ears, and heart in wise and insightful ways regarding the situation (Proverbs 2:6).

If, after praying, you sense that you are supposed to lovingly confront the other person, ask God to clothe you with compassion, kindness, humility, gentleness, patience, and love (Colossians 3:12, 14).

Step #2:

The purpose of loving confrontation is to compassionately point your wayward sister back to Jesus.

[Pointer finger: (*pointing up*) Help me point her to You, Jesus.]

The purpose of your conversation is *not* to hit a sister with your measuring stick of shame, to be "right," to cause church-wide conflict, or to produce embarrassment. The hope is for the wanderer to turn away from sin and turn back *to Jesus* for repentance and restoration (2 Corinthians 7:10; Galatians 6:1).

Ask God to equip and empower you so that whatever you say and do helps this person see the grace, love, and kindness of Jesus (Colossians 3:17).

Step #3:

Go to your sister in private and graciously show her the sin, speaking the truth in love.

[Middle finger: Speak.]

Using Ephesians 4:15 as your guide, prepare the words you hope to share. Speak directly to the person about your concerns, not to your small group as a "prayer request." Consider the best time, location, approach, and mode of communication. Whenever possible, speak face-to-face rather than by email or a phone call. This is not the time to use social media, texts, or for goodness sake—snap chat!

When you do "pull up a chair" to talk with your sister, start the conversation by assuring her that you are *for her.* You may want to use phrases or statements such as:

🌼 *"If your house were on fire, I wouldn't be a good friend if I stood back and watched it burn. As hard as it is to talk about this, I care for you and don't want to watch your house go up in flames."*

🌼 *"I know this is uncomfortable, but if the roles were reversed, I would want you to bring it up with me."*

🌼 *"You are important to me. I don't want you to look back years from now and wonder why I wasn't a caring sister in Christ to you and instead stood by and said nothing."*

Step #4:

Focus on the Truth of God's Word.

[Ring finger: Truth.]

Ask specific questions to confirm details/defuse the situation. Tenderly point out the sin. Lovingly show her Scripture that applies to her circumstances. Be careful not to share your personal opinion or what the world says is appropriate. Share the *truth*.

Your friend may respond with rationalization ("it's not that big of a deal, you're overreacting"), judgment ("who are you to judge me, I've seen you do worse!"), or outright denial.

Remember, your role is to speak the truth in love. Leave her response and the results in God's hands.

Step #5:

Love well.

[Pinky finger: Love.]

Wrap the conversation in love. Remind your dear sister of God's unfailing love, and your love for her too.

Be sure to keep your "glasses of grace" on long after the initial conversation. Follow up with a phone call, note in the mail, or small token of affection. Even if the conversation went differently than you had planned, *love*.

Love says:

❀ *"You're right, I'm not perfect either. Let's journey together."*

❀ *"I'm not going anywhere. I love you, I'm for you, and I'm committed to helping however I can."*

❀ *"Your house is on fire; I'm coming in after you!"*

❀ *"I love you enough to have these hard, awkward conversations."*

Let's review:

God gave *me* another chance to risk a friendship for His sake. Another friend's marriage was troubled, and she had reconnected with an old boyfriend on Facebook. At first, they were just "catching up," and then things took a more serious turn. She and her old "soul mate" began writing long and detailed notes to each other every day. Very quickly, their spark turned to heated flames. How could I stand by and watch as her home life and family burned to the ground?

Did I love her enough to take the risk that our friendship might not survive?

I pulled up another chair and told her the truth as I saw it, wrapped in love. This time was different. This time my friend listened, even though my manner of speaking was shaky and less than perfect. Thankfully, she soon removed herself from the budding, illicit relationship with her ex-boyfriend, and confessed everything. My friend and her husband worked extremely hard to get their marriage back on track, and their family was saved. Thank God!

 Is there a relationship or situation that needs your personal care and attention? Do you love this person enough to "speak the truth in love"? Use the space below to write a prayer to God. Ask God to use you to speak the truth in love to this sister so she too might *live full* and *walk free*.

PART FOUR:
Lost and Found

> **Memory Verse:** You were washed, you were sanctified, you were justified in the name of the Lord Jesus Christ and by the Spirit of our God.
>
> —1 Corinthians 6:11b

A few years ago, our family decided we'd stop for lunch at Wendy's every Sunday after church. At first, we went through the drive-thru, where we were usually greeted—or grunted at—by an older lady named Margo.

She had a deep, gravelly voice, glasses that she wore slid halfway down her nose, and a gold tooth in the front of her smile. Not that she smiled very much. She was a bit grumpy.

Okay, maybe a lot grumpy.

In fact, some of my family members (I won't name names) started to call her "Grumpy." As we'd pull up to the drive-thru, they'd say, "Oh no, look who's working today."

"What if we started to pray for her?" I said in my chipper way. (I don't understand why "chipper" is not always embraced with great enthusiasm by my family members, but I digress.)

"Ugh," said the family, but we all agreed to pray for Margo, asking that God would use us to show her what He is like. When we pray those kinds of prayers, God answers, and He began to soften each of our hearts toward crusty, crabby Margo.

Soon we started dining *inside* Wendy's each Sunday. And Margo started coming over to our booth to visit with us and give us free Frosties. Slowly, we developed a friendship. In fact, I can remember when we weren't going to be there the next week because of a mini vacation and Margo said, "Be sure to bring me pictures."

Sure enough, the next Sunday we went to Wendy's for lunch so we could visit with Margo and show her our vacation photos. Somehow, the gym at which we were members came up in our conversation that day. "Oh man, that one with all the pools and that huge water slide? I've dreamed about swimming there!"

Well, we didn't need a kick in the spiritual backside to get us to invite Margo to the gym. The next week, we brought in a week's membership pass for Margo, and invited her to spend the day at the pool with us.

I will never forget that day as long as I live. There was Margo, calling her sister in utter glee. "Girlfriend, you'll never guess where I am," she squealed into her phone. She flew down the water slide, screaming like a schoolgirl, hands in the air, whooping it up. "Grumpy" had been transformed into "Happy." It was a fantastic day at the pool, and our friendship with a lonely, troubled lady deepened into something special.

I must admit something though. Margo's life was "messy" when we met—she was a loud, proud sinner. I wondered—should we be spending so much time with her? Were we somehow "approving" of her sins by hanging out with her? Were we quietly saying her choices were A-OK?

The Corinthians wondered the same thing. How should they relate with those who were *outside* the church? Were they lending their stamp of approval to sin, just by hanging out with or working side by side with sinners?

They weren't the first or last believers to be confused on this topic. We are called to live *in* the world but not be *of* it (John 17:14–18). Many Christians over two millennia have interpreted this to mean that we need to exist in some kind of holy Ziploc bag, shutting out the fumes of sin and decay.

We have so many questions:

🍀 My unmarried, non-churchgoing neighbors are living together. Should I have them over for a barbecue?

🍀 My agnostic coworker drinks like a fish, but we share a love for Pinterest and DIY. Am I somehow saying her drinking is okay if I invite her over to chat about our latest projects?

🍀 The women in my book club sometimes want to read R-rated books. I'm uncomfortable with a few, not all, of our book club selections. Should I quit my current book club and join a Christians-only club?

The church members in Corinth would have had similar questions about how to live in fullness in their sin-marinated culture. Furthermore, they had misinterpreted Paul's lost letter (lost to us, not to them) as teaching them not to associate *at all* with flagrant sinners.

 I love how Paul clarified and offered a course correction in **1 Corinthians 5:9–10**. Those powerful verses are worth looking up again and summarizing below:

The Corinthian church members were all mixed up! Clearly they misunderstood Paul when they thought he didn't want them to associate with *any* immoral person. How could one live in Sin City and not be around sinners? You'd have to take the next boat out of town. Good thing Paul clarified!

Many of us make the same mistake today. We jump into our Christian bunkers or our airless Ziploc bags, and start shooting, heedless of whether our judge-y little bullets are wounding those Jesus came for, injuring those he loves. When we hold our Christian standard up to the world, and judge them against it, we wound people and injure the cause of Christ.

Let's be careful not to judge "the lost" because they sin differently than we do.

Jesus is our model for how to treat the "lost" people we interact with daily in our world. He was a "friend of tax collectors and sinners" (Matthew 11:19) and lived out a perfect balance of grace and truth with the folks He befriended during his thirty-three years on this Earth.

🌿 Digging Deeper

Jesus' friendship with tax collector Zacchaeus shows us the ideal way to interact with our neighbors, coworkers, and fellow book club members. As the chief tax collector, he was rolling in dough, most of which was gouged out of hardworking people who couldn't afford his hefty cut of the pie.

Everyone despised him—wouldn't you? It would be hard not to detest a guy who got rich off your back and the backs of your neighbors and friends. Yet Jesus was coming to him, to his town, Jericho. And when Zacchaeus climbed into that sycamore tree to watch Jesus above the crowd, he was about to meet the best friend he would ever have.

Read Luke 19:1–10. If you are familiar with this story, ask God to help you see these truth-filled words from a fresh perspective.

How did Jesus respond when He saw Zacchaeus (v. 5)?

Don't you love it! Zacchaeus looked down. Jesus looked up. And He said, "I see you. I know you. Let's share a meal."

How did all the people respond when they saw Jesus going to spend time with Zacchaeus (v. 7)?

Let's be careful not to judge "the lost" because they sin differently than we do.

What did Jesus say in verse 9 about Zacchaeus and his spiritual status?

How did Zacchaeus demonstrate his inward change through outward action (v. 8)?

Zacchaeus' response was amazing! He scrambled out of that tree into almost instant newness. It's as if he had been waiting all his life for someone to find him. Zacchaeus was all in—no messing around, no holding back. We can learn a lot from his openhearted response to Jesus and willingness to right his former wrongs. Zacchaeus was ready to *live full* and *walk free*!

What did Jesus say in verse 10 about His mission?

Jesus came to seek—to search for, hunt for, pursue, and go after—those who are lost. Jesus came to find us like he found Zacchaeus in a tree. He came to forgive us like he forgave a corrupt tax collector. He came to free us like he freed that little, lost man in Jericho. There is no one too far gone from His amazing grace!

Jesus also knew that acceptance didn't equal approval. He accepted Zacchaeus but never would have approved of the way he was cheating hardworking people in his town of Jericho.

We sometimes get that turned around, don't we? We disapprove of folks in their sinful behavior before we get a chance to accept them in Jesus' name.

As for Margo, I did accept her—to a point. I thought I was doing pretty good to know her name, pray for her, and give her waterslide passes for my gym. Yet I wasn't ready to go as far as Jesus went with Zacchaeus, not at first anyway.

When I hosted a home candle party in my house, I wasn't going to invite Margo. "God, it's one thing to visit her at work, but to invite her into my home, with all my friends?" Yikes. Just being honest here!

But God was not satisfied with my somewhat safe, sanitized level of involvement with His lost sheep, Margo. He nudged me in my spirit and made it plain I was to invite her into my home, with all my friends.

I see you. I know you. Let's share a meal.

Or, in the case of my candle party, finger foods and fruity non-alcoholic drinks.

That night, a miracle happened. My friend Julie took the time to sit with Margo and hear her story. She shared the gospel message with Margo, and Margo accepted Jesus as her Lord and Savior—at the candle party I almost didn't invite her to.

Jesus shows us how to find the lost, not fear them. He models that acceptance doesn't mean approval or endorsement.

Jesus sees into the trees of this world, into the drive-thru windows. He displays an eyes-wide-open way of life that seeks the lost. He really sees people like Zacchaeus, like Margo.

Do we?

Let's look up from our busyness, and our phones, *and our phones* (it bears repeating, you must admit!). Pay attention to the people with whom you share this beautiful, broken world.

 ## Apply It

The truth is this: Jesus loves the lost! Christ's love is so lavish that He pursues each person and celebrates when he or she is "found." (I'm picturing oodles of colorful confetti!) And as God's "tools," we've been personally invited to join Jesus' search-and-rescue mission to find His precious missing sheep (John 20:21). How are you doing at *knowing, living,* and *sharing* this truth?

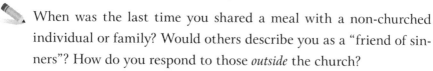 When was the last time you shared a meal with a non-churched individual or family? Would others describe you as a "friend of sinners"? How do you respond to those *outside* the church?

When do you worry about lending your stamp of approval to sin just by hanging out with or working side-by-side with sinners?

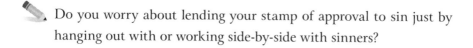 Is there someone in your sphere of influence you might invite to share a meal or cup of coffee?

May Christ's words to Zacchaeus become the very invitation we extend to a coworker, neighbor, family member, or fast food worker: *I see you. I know you. Let's share a meal.*

PART FIVE:
Brand Spanking New

> **Memory Verse:** You were washed, you were sanctified, you were justified in the name of the Lord Jesus Christ and by the Spirit of our God.
>
> —1 Corinthians 6:11b

One of my very favorite Bible stories is the one about the woman with the shameful past in Luke 7. I admire her bravery, her beautiful heart, and her willingness to be vulnerable—in spite of the critical judgment of others in her community. Unfortunately we don't even know her name—we only know her by her sinful choices: that she sold her body for money.[9]

What led this dear woman to become a prostitute? Was she a widow struggling to survive? Had she been mistreated as a child? Was she trying to fill the emptiness and loneliness as she looked for love in all the wrong places? The Bible doesn't say; we'd only be guessing.

What we do know is that reports of Jesus' ministry and teaching had somehow reached this woman, and she was eager to see the Savior. For her to shamelessly decide to join the banquet at Simon the Pharisee's house would not have been an easy decision. She was painfully aware of her soiled reputation around town. But she had heard of Jesus, and regardless of what others might say or think— she needed to spend time in His presence.

Turn to Luke 7:36–50 to join the Pharisee's dinner party. Read the story, and then answer the questions on the next page.

How was the unnamed woman described in verse 37? How would you feel being identified in such a way?

How did Simon the Pharisee respond when he saw the woman interacting with Jesus (v. 39)?

What was Jesus' comeback to Simon in verse 43? Circle the correct answer below.

"You have _____ correctly," Jesus answered.

Extended grace	Worshiped	Esteemed
Accepted her	Loved	Guessed
Believed	Judged	Responded

What question did Jesus ask Simon in verse 44?

Oh those pride-filled Pharisees and their snooty shaming sticks! When Simon saw her, he saw a sinful woman, period. He didn't see God's dearly loved daughter, a "lost sheep" looking for home. Instead, he labeled *this woman* by her past and her poor choices.

Unclean. Unwanted. Unworthy.

But Jesus missed nothing. He saw *her*.

Sure, He knew *exactly* what kind of woman had just washed his feet with her tears—one with a laundry list of sexual sins in her past.

But Jesus also knew that who she was at one time was *not* who she was now. Her past did not define her, but her relationship with Jesus *did*. And by the time this woman left Simon's home, He had transformed *everything* for her with four straightforward words—"your sins are forgiven" (Luke 7:48).

This gorgeous story of grace helps us understand what was going on with the Corinthians. Many of these Sin City citizens had a story just like the woman at Simon's house. Among the church members, noted Paul, were brothers and sisters who had been sexually immoral, worshiped idols, and struggled with drunkenness and greed.

"And that is what *some of you were*. But you were washed, you were sanctified, you were justified in the name of the Lord Jesus Christ and by the Spirit of our God" (1 Corinthians 6:11, emphasis added).

Some of you were like that, but not anymore.

Digging Deeper

Yesterday we learned about Zacchaeus, who had been a despised member of the Jericho community. Until that beautiful day when Jesus saw him in a tree, Zacchaeus had lived his life on his own terms—selfish, greedy, and callous to the needs of others.

But when he encountered Jesus, *everything* changed. Zacchaeus received a new heart, a new mind, even a new purpose. We witnessed how his brand new heart took action immediately when he began to repay those from whom he had stolen—and refund not only the amount he had taken but four times as much.

Unlike Zacchaeus, however, the Corinthians had forgotten their *new* identities. Some were slip sliding away back to their old worldly ways—and they needed a wake-up call. So fresh on the heels of addressing lawsuits among believers—*oh vey!*—Paul recapped what happened to these men and women when they received Christ, an experience that separated them from their non-religious neighbors and friends.

 Read 1 Corinthians 6:9–11. Write the three words of identity Paul shared in verse 11.

After listing some of their previous sins, Paul reminded the believers that Jesus separated them from their past life. *Some of you were like that, but not anymore.* In addition, Paul highlighted God's powerful accomplishment in making them (and us!) *new* people:

We are washed. In Christ, we are scrubbed clean of our previous sins. Like the woman with the alabaster jar, we are showered in grace, bathed in mercy.

 How might knowing you are squeaky clean in Christ help you to live differently?

We are sanctified. In Christ, we are set apart for God. Do you recall this reminder from the opening of Paul's Corinthian correspondence? Maybe you even took my challenge from video lesson 1 and wrote an "S" on your hand?

The Greek word used in 1 Corinthians 6:11 is the same Greek word for *sanctified* we looked at in 1 Corinthians 1:2. We are called to be saints in our sinful cities! A sanctified woman should stand out from the crowd.

We are justified. In Christ, we are pronounced "not guilty" for our sins, declared innocent before God. Per The Message paraphrase, *God got us out of the mess we're in and restored us to where He always wanted us to be. And He did it by means of Jesus Christ.*[10]

The truth for the Corinthians and us: once we accept Christ's amazing invitation, we are generously given everything we need to live a full, free, pleasing-to-God life. We are washed. Sanctified. Justified. Christ followers should differ from the crooked, shady folks around them.

Paul is saying, "Hey, friends, you just simply cannot continue on in your old habits. Your new hearts should be making a visible difference in the way you live your lives." You have a new identity in Christ, and this new identity requires new and *appropriate* behavior. (My kids' least favorite word—*appropriate*. They know a "mom lecture" is in store when I start talking about *appropriate* behavior.)

But clearly, the Corinthian brothers and sisters desperately needed yet another lecture from Paul as to who they now were in Christ—*some of you were like that, but not anymore.* In fact, can you believe Paul had to remind them of this truth yet again in future correspondence? Can anyone say "thick skull"?

 Turn to 2 Corinthians 5:17 and write it below. Circle the word(s) describing our unique identity in Christ.

I love the word *new*! It's from a Greek word describing something that is brand new or recently made. It also carries the idea of something that is superior. This means when Jesus Christ came into your life, you were made *brand, spanking new*![11] The new you is better-quality than the old you! In fact, you are so new that this verse calls you a new "creation."

Sweet friend, in Christ, everything about you is new! You're not an altered, revised version of what you used to be. You are an absolutely brand-new woman! You are completely disconnected from the person you once were before Christ. This is more than turning over a new leaf—you've been given a new life!

 How do you feel knowing that in Christ you are *brand, spanking new*?

Sometimes, just remembering what God has done for us both inspires us and helps put things into larger perspective. Paul wanted the Corinthians and you and me to take our calling seriously—to leave behind the old habits and the bad patterns and to live in the newness of our holy-fueled lives.

This is more than turning over a new leaf— you've been given a new life!

Take Zacchaeus. He was short in stature but tall in grace. He took his newness seriously. He was genuinely, earnestly, truly a new man. Can you imagine the faces of those he had swindled as he practically threw heaps of money at them? And maybe he laughed with joy at their stunned expressions. "Hey," I can hear him saying. "I'm just not that guy anymore."

Take the ~~sinful~~ forgiven woman at Simon's banquet, the one with the beautiful, costly gift. She did not mess around either. She took her newness seriously. She was truly a new woman. Yeah, Simon and his silly, puffy pals wanted to keep her in her old life with their pinched lips and squinty eyes and shaming sticks. But maybe she was too busy pouring out her love at the feet of Jesus to even notice. "Hey," I can hear her saying. "I'm just not that girl anymore."

Apply It

If you are a Christian, how have you noticed changes in your thoughts, attitudes, or actions since you started following Jesus?

Turn back to the cross example on page 16. Reflect on your life BC (before Christ), when/how you were introduced to Jesus, and how your life is now new and different AC (after Christ). You may want to add washed, sanctified, and justified to your AC list!

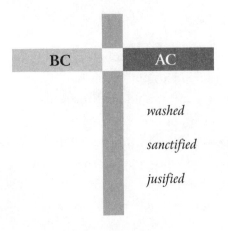

washed

sanctified

jusified

Do you regularly reflect on the new person you now are in Jesus Christ, or do you still look at yourself through the eyes of the past? Do you see yourself through "glasses of grace" and celebrate Jesus' changes in you, or do you fault-find yourself to pieces?

Spend time in prayer thanking God for His transformational work in your life, and ask Him to help you view yourself as the *new* creation He has called you to be.

Video Lesson Three:
NEW HEARTS, OLD HABITS

Use the space below to note anything that stands out to you from the video lesson. You may also choose to take notes on a separate sheet of paper.

Use the following questions as a guide for group discussion:

1. What stood out to you in today's video teaching? Any new insights?

2. When was the last time you found yourself in a "sticky situation"? How did you respond? Anything you might do differently next time?

3. Reread 1 Corinthians 4:6. Have you ever been "puffy" or picked up your "measuring stick" to evaluate, critique, or judge? Looking back, how might you have responded in a more loving way?

4. Review Paul's message regarding the lost in 1 Corinthians 5:9–10. How do you most often respond to those *outside* the church? Have you shared a meal with a non-churched individual or family recently? Do you ever worry about approving of sin just by hanging out with "sinners"?

5. Read aloud this week's memory verse, 1 Corinthians 6:11b. What does this verse mean to you? How should your attitudes and actions be affected by knowing, living, and sharing this truth?

CHAPTER FOUR

Sex in the Sinful City

Prayer:

O Lord, I acknowledge You as my Creator and Maker. Thank You for knitting me together perfectly in my mother's womb, and for the promise that I am fearfully and wonderfully made. Forgive me for the times I fuss and fret about my outside appearance. How it must grieve Your heart when I focus on my flaws and faults. Give me eyes to see myself as You see me. Teach me Your truth about my body, my worth, my sexuality. May my beliefs and behaviors be based on Your Word and not on the messages from the world. God, please reveal any ways I have missed the mark. My desire is to *live full* and *walk free* so that I can reflect Your love and grace in the midst of our lost, hurting, and broken world. In the sanctifying, liberating name of Jesus I pray. Amen.

PART ONE:
Birds & Bees & Beliefs

Memory Verse: You are not your own; you were bought at a price. Therefore honor God with your bodies.

—1 Corinthians 6:19b–20

Let's talk about sex.

Are you blushing already—wondering why a simple Midwestern Bible teacher would bring up such a subject? Are you tempted to flip the pages forward, thinking this topic is not your issue? Or is your heart glad that someone, finally, is talking about the act and the feelings that have caused so much joy and so much pain in our world, in your life, and in the lives of those you love?

I know—it can be awkward, especially with family members.

I remember being on a road trip with one of my boys when the oh-so-mortifying topic of sex came up—sort of. It's not like I took advantage of a captive audience and began waxing forth on the birds and the bees. Not with my son in the back seat, and my mother in the front.

The topic came up in a sideways kind of way, as it often does. My son had to use the bathroom, and we were on a tight timeline to get where we were going.

"Just go in a cup," my mom said, already rummaging around for the ideal porta-potty.

What? No.

"Uh, no way!" I said, swerving the van just a teensy bit as I glanced at my boy through the rearview mirror. "Do not take that thing out in this car! Keep your 'private part' in your pants!" (Though I bravely used the anatomically correct term.) My son's cheeks turned a ripe shade of grapefruit as he stared out the window, hoping for a gas station sign to appear quickly.

That's just one example of how even a little talk of body parts can make us feel uncomfortable, not to mention when we approach the actual subject of sexuality. It's interesting that in our sex-obsessed culture, we can be quite shy when it comes to talking about sex. One friend said she's never heard the topic discussed even once by her pastor after sitting under his teaching for twelve years.

Paul was not that pastor. Thankfully, he was very open about sex, bringing it up often with his flock in various assemblies of the early church, including Corinth. While our society is sex-obsessed and corrupt, what we face in comparison to Corinth is mild, my friends, *mild*. Talk about *Sex in the City*!

Let's review what we've learned about the city, people, and culture of Corinth—especially with regard to sexual immorality.

You'll recall, Corinth was the Sin City of its day. "Corinth had a worldwide reputation for being a 'party city' and a center for 'sexual freedom' . . . The entire city was devoted to the sex industry; therefore any kind of sex was considered acceptable and fair," writes one scholar.[1]

In ancient Corinth, a little girl would have thought it was nothing that her mommy and daddy went to worship at the temple of Aphrodite, the goddess of love. She would not have blinked to see prostitutes walking down the city streets. It would have been routine for the men in her life —daddy, grandpa, big brother—to use prostitutes (male or female), whether at one of the temples, a brothel, or even at a Greek dinner party.

Greek society shouted a message that life was all about pleasure and feeding the appetites of your body. If you wanted it, you could have it. *Anything* goes.

Two important beliefs, or slogans, were popular in the Corinthian culture during Paul's time. If there were bumper stickers on

Corinthian chariots, instead of "Got goat milk?" "Kiss my gyro," or "What happens in Corinth stays in Corinth," the bumper stickers would declare: *"I have the right to do anything."*

This belief was well known and deeply engrained in their thinking, especially among the wealthy. Remember, anything and everything was permissible in Sin City. As well as: *"Food for the Stomach and the Stomach for Food."*

The Greeks believed the body and soul were divided. The body was bad; the soul was good. Your body has appetites, so go ahead and feed them; it won't affect your soul.

They also thought food and sex were parallel. If you are hungry, eat. If you have the urge to have sex, do it! Bodies are driven by pleasure, so please your body in whatever way you want to.

Disastrously, these false beliefs were shaping the behaviors of the Corinthian church members. Many precious children of God were being blinded by the skewed standards all around them.

> *For many women, living in our sex-crazed culture has drastically warped their ability to live full and walk free.*

Can we relate? Sex is still one of Satan's favorite schemes. Clearly, he's using sexual sin to hook our culture, just like he did Corinth. Porn is rampant, sexting among teens is commonplace, and there's even pro-adultery websites that beguile discontented, broken husbands and wives. TV, films, and the Internet offer a constant eyeful of near-naked and naked bodies. We can't even go to the grocery store for salad fixings without seeing sexual images on the covers of checkout magazines.

For many women, living in our sex-crazed culture has drastically warped their ability to *live full* and *walk free*. Are you curious about what Paul said to the Corinthians? About what his letter says to you?

Digging Deeper

Paul, per usual, tackled the issues head on. Let's unearth more of Paul's message to that wild, wayward church in Corinth.

Read 1 Corinthians 6:12–17. Be on the lookout for ways the beliefs of the culture were impacting the behavior of the church members, and jot down your insights below.

The Corinthian Christ followers were being duped! They were totally bedazzled by Satan's sparkly lures and society's glare. The church members knew the truth, but they allowed their sexually distorted backgrounds and the common cultural messages to shape their behavior. Before long, the saints were visiting prostitutes again and joining in on sexual activities at the temples—and fellow church members didn't blink an eye.

Rather than the church impacting the culture, the culture was impacting the church.

Sound familiar? We fall for the same thing in our day and age. It's so easy to allow the messages of our media and culture to shape our thoughts, feelings, and actions—particularly when it comes to sexuality.

Let's start by reflecting on where women learn about the "birds and the bees" for the first time in today's culture, and circle your response(s) below.

Magazines	Internet	Youth group/church
School	Older sibling	YouTube
Bible	Mom and Dad	Painful situations
Playground	Cable TV	Pornography
Music	Social media	Peers
Other:		

Unfortunately, the reality is too many children learn about sex from everyone *but* their parents. Focus on the Family shares, "Playground slang and obscenity, a distorted description of intercourse from the tough kid up the street, or worst of all, a look at some pornographic material on cable TV or the Internet often provides a child's first jarring glimpse of sex."[2]

You may remember from my message at the beginning of this book, I speak from the heart on this sensitive issue. As a very little girl, I was introduced to the world's definition of beauty and sexuality through risqué girlie magazines. As I grew into my teens, my influences changed. I learned about sex by watching *The Last American Virgin* and other R-rated '80s movies on HBO while I was babysitting. I thought sex was a casual, glittering thing, and to be sexy and wanted was the most important prize in the world. Unfortunately, my beliefs about sex—by then distorted into something truly sad—turned into damaging behaviors. I acted out what I thought to be true about sex—and the consequences were shattering.

Here's my lesson learned: Our beliefs shape our behavior. Wrong thinking equals wrong actions. Every. Single. Time. If our desire is to experience Christ's *fullness* and *freedom*, we must make sure our beliefs are based on the truth of the Word of God.

 Look up John 8:32 and write it below. Circle the benefit of *knowing* the truth.

Apply It

Before we go any further, an important word. Please know, as I was preparing this chapter, I carefully considered how to best communicate this crucial message with sensitivity, wisdom, authenticity, and grace.

Hopefully by now, you know my heart.

I'm definitely not shaking my shaming stick at you. *Never.* Trust me: I would be the very last person to judge anyone. My hope is to share Christ's message of truth and grace, fullness and freedom; sprinkled with lots of love. And remember, with Jesus, it's not "shame on you" but "shame off you."[3]

When we talk about sexuality, we automatically come with our own baggage. Maybe your baggage is light—a makeup bag or tote bag, perhaps. Or maybe, like me, your baggage is more like a travel trunk of sexual disgrace. If you've picked up any baggage on life's journey—whether a petite tote or an extra-large travel case—first, please know: you are not the only one.

I often meet women who are weighed down by the pain and humiliation of their sexual pasts, even many years later. I've shed tears with countless friends who expressed feeling intense guilt for premarital sex, abortions, affairs, or other sexual sin. I've walked with beautiful women who disclosed their excruciating stories of childhood sexual victimization. They know it's not their fault and that they should "move on." They've tried to live forgiven and free, yet they can't shake the shame.

> *When we talk about sexuality, we automatically come with our own baggage.*

This I know based on the authority of God's Word: no matter what you have done, or what has been done to you—Jesus Christ came so you might *live full* and *walk free.*

Now in case you are thinking, "But, Cindy, practically speaking, what does that mean? I *want* fullness and freedom in my life, but *how?*"

Oh dear one, it takes faith, but I believe it can be as straightforward as A, B, C.

A – *Always start with Jesus.*

Acknowledge your pain to Him. Admit your sins and wrongdoings. Express your hurts and need for healing. Kneel before His feet in worship.

Depending on your past, you may want to invite a trusted godly friend, your small group leader, or a Christian counselor to join you on this journey. Ask her to help you give your cares and concerns to the One who is our Healer, Shame-lifter, Rescuer, and Redeemer.

Personally, after I accepted Christ, I wrote all of my previous shameful choices and experiences on a helium balloon with a permanent marker (okay, so it took two balloons with small handwriting). After confessing my sins, I prayerfully let the balloons go. Up, up, and away the sin-covered balloons went into the cloud-filled sky. As I released the balloons, I also released my burdens to the One who is our Burden Bearer (Isaiah 53:4). I experienced freedom like never before!

B – *Believe that what God's Word says is truth.*

Keep in mind, as a Christ follower, you have the mind of Christ (1 Corinthians 2:16). Spend time daily thinking God's truth-filled thoughts on your past, present, and future. Here are some power-packed verses to get you started: Psalm 32:3–5; Romans 8:1; Galatians 5:1; and 1 John 1:9.

Remember, our beliefs shape our behavior. Let's believe *truth*.

C – *Choose peace.*

How I treasure the words Jesus spoke to the no-longer-sinful woman from Luke 7:48. Read them aloud from the Amplified Bible below.

> *Jesus said to the woman, "Your faith [in Me] has saved you; go in peace [free from the distress experienced because of sin]."*

Circle Jesus's offer to the Luke 7 woman, and to you and me too.

As you go about your daily life, make choices that will lead you toward peace. Will hanging out with that old boyfriend at his apartment lead to peace? Will sharing intimate details of past partners with others lead to peace? Will rehearsing the sins of your youth lead to peace?

Sweet friend, let's choose the path toward peace. Ultimately, the peace we are all searching for and longing for will never be found in a steamy relationship, self-condemnation, or social media. His name is Jesus.

 Write out the ABCs of overcoming the guilt and regret of past sin, sexual or otherwise. Shape them into a prayer as you scribble them below.

PART TWO:
Survey Says

> **Memory Verse:** You are not your own; you were bought at a price. Therefore honor God with your bodies.
>
> —1 Corinthians 6:19b–20

I recently asked on Facebook, "When it comes to sex and our body, what are some current popular beliefs from our culture?" Here are the widely held ideas I crowd-sourced:

- ❀ You want a casual, no-strings-attached relationship? No problem! (i.e., "friends with benefits")

- ❀ Waiting is old-fashioned. Get with the times.

- ❀ It's my body. I can do what I want.

- ❀ Sex is just sex. It's not connected to intimacy and feelings.

- ❀ Your identity is in your sexuality.

- ❀ Sex is nobody's business but mine.

- ❀ YOLO—you only live once.

- ❀ Porn is no big deal—everyone looks at it.

What about your city or town? What cultural messages would Paul hear and witness if he came to live in your neighborhood for a year and a half?

Whether you live in Las Vegas or Mayberry, I'm betting Paul would notice the same kinds of things he did in Corinth, because we all live in Sin City to one degree or another. We exist in a strikingly comparable culture to the church in Corinth, a world of confusion and compulsion. We too live in a world where anything and everything goes.

Perhaps we used to live in a somewhat sanitized society, where wholesomeness and purity were at least valued on the face of things, if not behind closed doors. But it's not true anymore. Increasingly, we live in a place and time marked by the exact opposite values. And worse—all the hedonism and toxic garbage are only a click away, no matter where our brick and mortar homes actually sit. (Sometimes, we don't even have to click on anything purposefully and we still get filth right in our faces. Recently I opened an innocent email and was mortified to see a pornographic picture popping out at me. Yikes!)

It's pretty obvious we live in an age when things are getting worse, not better. As I write these words, our world is showing its brokenness in heart-wrenching ways. The global sex trade is exploding: trafficking women and children for sexual exploitation is the fastest growing crime in the world. This, despite the fact that international law and the laws of 134 countries criminalize sex trafficking. About two million children are abused and oppressed every year in the global commercial sex trade, and women and girls make up 98 percent of victims. It's overwhelming just to recite those statistics.[4]

Our own American culture is unraveling fast too. I see the clues everywhere. In Corinth, there were methods of spreading the decadence, such as messages in the sand left by the footprints of temple prostitutes. Today our "messages in the sand" are different, but the message is the same: *"Follow me. If it feels right, it must be right. What's the big deal?"*

But it is a *big deal*, friends. And so is falling for each and every one of the deceptive beliefs the enemy uses to lure and entice us off the path of God's best. Our beliefs shape our behavior, and if we are going to *live full* and *walk free* in this sin-soaked world, we must be intentional about fixing our thoughts, not our feelings, on the power-filled Word of God.

Digging Deeper

How did Paul respond to the Corinthians' distorted ideas about sex? He challenged both their beliefs and their behavior, offsetting their twisted ideas about sexual relations with truth.

Paul wrote a letter to the church in Thessalonica while he was living in Corinth.

 Read 1 Thessalonians 4:1–12 and write down what Paul said to this young Jesus community regarding sexual desires and activities.

Paul had taught the Thessalonians how to live pure lives in their impure world—and now he was urging them to put into practice what they'd learned. No doubt Paul coached the Corinthians in the same way. He loved them! He wanted them to *live full* and *walk free*. Yet he was aware of their culture of nonstop bad behavior, dedication to false gods, and wild excesses. Can you picture Paul, during his midmorning teaching sessions with the Corinthians, leaning in and saying:

🌿 God created you male and female in His image with dignity, equality, value, and worth! Men and women, you are different and yet you complement one another! (See Genesis 1:27–28.)

🌿 God created sex. God made your bodies "very good" with "male and female" parts and pleasures. God fashioned sex as a gift for you to steward and enjoy. (See Genesis 2:24–25.)

❧ God prohibits all sexual relationships outside of marriage. No exceptions! (See Exodus 20:14.)

Really? *No* sex outside of marriage? How come?

"Sex functions like the fire in a fireplace. God wants the fire to burn hot and passionate inside the fireplace of marriage, where it brings light, heat, warmth, and intimacy. But when the fire is taken out of the fireplace to places it shouldn't be, it destroys, and its purpose is also destroyed," writes author Chip Ingram.[3]

> *God sets sexual boundaries as if to say, "Sweet daughter, I want you to have the best."*

God sets sexual boundaries as if to say, "Sweet daughter, I want you to have the best. I want to protect you. I want to provide for you. Your sexuality is not just an action or an appetite. And sex is definitely not a way to find, earn, or keep love. Sex matters. You matter. Trust Me on this, beloved. I don't want you to get burned."

 Do you know someone who has been burned by taking the "fire" of sex out of the "fireplace"?

Unfortunately, we know how it went down in Corinth: The church members allowed the loud cultural messages and their sexually distorted backgrounds to dictate their views instead of God. Not long after Paul left for Ephesus, the Corinthians began to slide back to their old ways. Many of the married men returned to the practice of enjoying sex outside of their marriage bed. Some church members even believed they would receive spiritual blessings from having sex with temple prostitutes! The Christ followers were following the world instead of following God's Word. Paul couldn't stand back and do nothing while his brothers and sisters were allowing their old beliefs and behaviors to impact their new relationship with Christ.

 Read 1 Corinthians 6:18–20. Summarize Paul's passionate plea below.

**Apply It**

If our desire is to *live full* and *walk free*, we must distinguish God's truth from the mixed-up messages of the world. To help, let's compare what "the world says" versus "what the Word of God says." As in Chapter 2, use the chart beginning below and ending on page 142 to write down the current messages we receive from our culture (the world), and then note what God's Word says about each topic. I'll get us started.

TOPIC	WORLD SAYS	GOD'S WORD SAYS
Sexual past	*If I've already been sexually active, it's too late to be pure. My promiscuous past labels me.*	*If we confess our sins, he is faithful and just and will forgive us our sins and purify us from all unrighteousness.* 1 John 1:9
Purpose of our body		1 Corinthians 6:19–20

TOPIC	WORLD SAYS	GOD'S WORD SAYS
Marriage		Genesis 2:24–25; Proverbs 5:18–19; Hebrews 13:4
Sexuality		Genesis 1:26–28
Extramarital affairs		Proverbs 6:32; Matthew 19:19
Pornography		Matthew 5:27–28; Ephesians 5:3

TOPIC	WORLD SAYS	GOD'S WORD SAYS

Use the last row above to "make your own." Fill in a topic you sense the enemy uses to distort the truth about God's design for sexuality in today's sex-saturated culture.

 As you reflect on this chart, do you have any new insights? Any areas where you need a mind-shift?

Remember, the truth will set you and me and our confused culture free. Regardless of what the world says, commit to *knowing, living,* and *sharing* what God's Word says about sexuality and the purpose of our God-designed bodies.

 Write a prayer for your community, asking God to open eyes, ears, and hearts to follow the Word wholeheartedly rather than following the lures and schemes of the world.

PART THREE:
Flee!

> **Memory Verse:** You are not your own; you were bought at
> a price. Therefore honor God with your bodies.
>
> —1 Corinthians 6:19b–20

"Call me anytime, from anywhere, and I'll be there to pick you up. No questions asked."

Over and over again, my mom spoke these grace-filled words to me: as a youngster, teenybopper, and college student. Who am I kidding—her offer still stands today! My mom knows me well, and somehow my spunky personality was drawn like a magnet to situations where trouble lurked. In her great love, she wanted me prepared with an "exit strategy" tucked in my back pocket. The time to plan my way out was not when I found myself in a pickle. Mom wanted there to be no doubt what to do—call for help and get outta there *fast*!

Now that I'm the mama bird, with one bird launched from the nest and three more not far behind, I hear my sweet mom's familiar words leaving my lips often: *"Call me anytime, from anywhere, and I'll be there to pick you up. No questions asked."* Don't get me wrong—my kids are good kids. But for all of us, regardless of our upbringing, it's easy to find ourselves in circumstances that challenge our integrity. We *all* need plans and strategies, escape routes and exits, so that we can *live full* and *walk free* in our licentious landscape.

The same was true for the Christ followers in fast-and-loose Corinth. Let's peel back the layers of Pastor Paul's letter as he carefully and gracefully presented essential truths for sexual freedom.

Digging Deeper

 Revisit 1 Corinthians 6:12–20, focusing specifically on verse 18. Write Paul's candid and clear command below:

The Greek word for *sexual immorality* is *porneia*, which is where we get our English word *pornography*. It means "any or all kinds of sexual activity outside of marriage."[6] *Porneia* refers not only to visiting prostitutes, brothels, or having a mistress on the side; the word refers to *any* kind of sex outside of marriage. Yes, *any*.

Kevin DeYoung defines *porneia* this way: "think about things that would make you furious and heartbroken if you found out someone was doing them with your husband."[7] Not married? Think about a close friend, your mom, or your child.

Perhaps you're wondering if (fill in the blank) is considered *porneia*. Well, would you want someone to do that activity with your husband or your mom? You should be able to answer your own question.

Incredibly, this word *porneia* occurs twenty-six times in the New Testament. Since they talked about sex so openly in the early church, we should talk about it openly in our churches too!

 Look up the following verses and record what you learn about sexual immorality:

1 Thessalonians 4:3

Colossians 3:5

Ephesians 5:3

Not even a hint, Paul said. This must have blown the early church members' minds. They were steeped in sexual temptation like a tea bag of Earl Grey submerged in hot water. Yet Paul's charge was crystal clear: they—*we*—have been instructed to live without a whiff of *porneia*, even in our sex-crazed culture.

But, *how*? How do we live a sexually pure life in a culture polluted through and through? Paul's strategy is simple, short, and effective.

 Write Paul's four-letter strategy out below.

If you are tempted to engage in sexual immorality, run like your house is on fire. Flee!

Yes, flee! Run for the hills! Pronto!

Paul even used the present imperative tense which could be translated, "Keep on fleeing!" or "Make it your habit to flee!"[8]

If you are tempted to engage in sexual immorality, run like your house is on fire. Flee!

Do not try to overcome it; do not try to ignore it; do not try to rationalize it. Do not say:

"We'll be more careful this time."

"We've both been married before. What do you expect?"

"We're consenting adults. What's the big deal?"

"Everybody's doing it!"

Paul's command is loud and strong: Flee. F-L-E-E. Flee!

Let's look at a real-life biblical example of fleeing from sexual temptation: the life of Joseph. Quick recap: Joseph's big brothers hated him and sold him into slavery; he ended up working for Potiphar, otherwise known as the Egyptian pharaoh's assassin. Potiphar put Joseph in charge of everything he owned (see Genesis 37; 39.)

Let's pick up the story by **reading Genesis 39:6–7.**

145

Enter Mrs. Potiphar, who apparently had a huge attraction for Joseph. The Bible tells us he was attractive, and we can probably guess that Potiphar didn't marry her for her brains and personality. Slinky Mrs. P would have made a good cast member on "Real Housewives of Ancient Egypt." The first episode might have included the part where she propositions Joseph:

"Come to bed with me!" she says. (Not exactly subtle.)

 But Joseph flexed his resistance muscles. **Read verses 8–9** and record his response.

I love how Joseph's desire to please God was forefront in his mind. But Potiphar's wife was not taking no for an answer. She begged Joseph to sleep with her, day after day. Then one day she literally snatched him—grabbing his robe and demanding he have sex with her.

 How did Joseph respond (v. 12)?

When faced with sexual temptation, Joseph fled. He bolted, leaving his clothing in her hands, and ran, not just out of the room *but* out the door! *Flee, Joseph, flee!*

Joseph is the perfect example of someone who loved God more than his sexual desires. The next time someone says, "All men look at porn," or "Men can't help themselves. It's how they're wired," let's remember Joseph. He actually did what Paul tells us to do: flee at the first sign of sexual impropriety! You see, *all* may be tempted, but *all* have a choice. Big difference. Any time you or I are tempted by sexual activity outside of marriage—our exit strategy is simple: we need to flee!

Apply It

I wonder where this message finds you today, sister? Are you involved in relationships where boundaries are being crossed? Are you drawn to racy movies, iffy novels, or sex-infused online streaming? When it comes to sexual sin or sensual choices, please don't try to justify it. Don't even get close to it. Flee, girlfriend, flee!

If Paul visited your house or mine, I think we might hear him say:

- If you're reading trashy romance novels that elevate our culture's twisted view of sex and plant illicit images in your head—please stop!

- If you are married and getting too close to your handsome new coworker—end it immediately.

- If you're watching porn with your partner to spice things up, please zap it off.

And if I could visit your house, I'd cup your hands in mine and say:

Sweet friend, your God is for you. Sex is a gift from Him to be enjoyed in His perfect timing. Take it from someone who lived the world's way: sex outside of God's boundaries leads to heartache, rejection, and shame. You matter. Your sexuality matters. God made sex to be beautiful and pleasurable. Today is the perfect day for a fresh start. The "rules" God has given for sex are to protect your heart as well as your body. You are so loved. Trust Him.

My mom's grace-filled words were helpful to me as a child, but God's wisdom is powerful and effective. He says:

"Call to me and I will answer you . . ." (Jeremiah 33:3).

"[I] will never let you down; [I'll] never let you be pushed past your limit; [I'll] always be there to help you come through it (1 Corinthians 10:13 MSG).

If you are faced with a sexually tempting situation, call out to Him! He is for you. And remember, regardless of your past choices and experiences, you are meant to *live full* and *walk free*.

PART FOUR:
Temple Talk

Memory Verse: You are not your own; you were bought at a price. Therefore honor God with your bodies.

—1 Corinthians 6:19b–20

"Cindy Stille is a fat red cow."

These seven words would define me for the next two decades. Scrawled on the chipped bathroom door of the girls' restroom at my high school, these words attached to me like a sticky nametag. "Hello, my name is Cindy. I'm a fat red cow."

I didn't know that the other kids would snicker about it for a time, and then forget; or that a janitor would scrape the words off and paint over them. If only he could have painted over my memory.

I didn't know the truth yet; that God calls me something very different—His daughter, the apple of His eye, a princess of great price. So I believed a bathroom stall scrawl and gave it tremendous power over my life and behavior. I allowed those words to chisel my worth and carve up my value. Whenever I thought about my body or my looks, I flashed back on those ugly etchings. *A fat red cow . . . uh huh, that's me.*

As the years went on, I appeared happy and self-confident on the outside. But beneath the cheery smile and bubbly personality was an insecure, injured young woman meticulously attempting to cover up the pain and striving to protect herself from ever being hurt or teased . . . again.

I wonder, can you relate? What untrue words have been spoken about you? Circle any/all words with which you can identify:

Useless	Good for Nothing	Worthless
Not good enough	Fat	Lazy
Disappointment	Stupid	Loser
Failure	Black sheep	Crazy
Clumsy	Ugly	Not wanted
Other:		

 Who said that to you? Do you remember where you picked up that lying label? Are you ready to take it off?

"Labels are awful," Lysa TerKeurst says. "They imprison us in categories that are hard to escape. Those labels start out as little threads of self-dissatisfaction but ultimately weave together into a straitjacket of self-condemnation."[9]

She's right. Lying labels *are* awful. And when we believe them—as we often do—we start to behave in a way that lines up with that false belief. If we think we are (fill in the blank), we will soon begin to act that way.

For example, if we believe our bodies are worthless, we will begin to conduct ourselves in that way: overeating, drinking too much, starving ourselves, or maybe even engaging in unhealthy sexual relations. I can't say this enough: our beliefs shape our behavior. To *live full* and *walk free*, we must have our beliefs based on the Word of God.

Digging Deeper

Refresh your memory by rereading the familiar words of **1 Corinthians 6:12–20**. Note what the passage teaches about the purpose of our body, and fill in the chart below:

OUR BODY IS . . .	OUR BODY ISN'T . . .

 Did you notice the word Paul used in verse 19 to describe our bodies? Write it below.

A temple, huh? Wow. As we've learned, temples were everywhere in Corinth. The Corinthians would have been as familiar with temples as a modern city dweller would be with skyscrapers, or a rural person would be with silos. Paul's words would have provided them with a very real visual image. Except this time, he was saying something different about temples.

As in shockingly different.

"Do you not know that *your bodies are temples of the Holy Spirit, who is in you, who you have received from God?*"

Say what? Are you seriously saying we are not to worship *at* the temple, but that we as individuals actually *are* the temple? Is our crazy Pastor Paul actually saying the Holy Spirit of God dwells within our flesh and skin and bones?

(Not to be confused with 1 Corinthians 3, when Paul talked about how collectively the church community was the temple. Remember, y'all?)

In fact, Paul used the word *naos* in the Greek, literally meaning "a temple or highly decorated shrine."[10] Upon reading Paul's words, his letter recipients would have instantly imagined what a temple looked like: domed ceilings, glossy columns, stonework floors, and exquisite woodwork overlaid with gold and silver. In other words, fancy. Elegant. Important.

Those words must have blown their minds! Remember, for the Corinthians, their warped beliefs were producing appalling behavior. Church members had bought into their city's slogan: "Food for the body, and the body for food." The way they were living out their beliefs was all about self-gratification. Prostitution was acceptable and having sex with someone other than your spouse was a conventional thing. Drinking to excess and gluttony was totally A-OK. Using and abusing your body was no big deal; besides, it didn't affect their soul, or so they thought. And now Paul was telling them their body is a temple, a sacred place, the place of the Holy Spirit? Wow.

Back in the '80s, when I was a teenage girl with bathroom scrawls etched in my spirit, I believed my body was shabby, too big, too much, and not enough. So I acted on those beliefs, developing eating disorders and substance abuse issues. I was promiscuous, and threw my body away like pearls before many swine.

My body talk was terrible, because I *believed* I was a fat red cow. Even after I surrendered my life to Jesus, and my actual physique became a shrine to the one true God, I struggled with poor body talk. I had not completely taken hold of the concept Paul taught the Corinthians: that my body carries with it the very Spirit of God. Gradually, I began to realize that this lousy body talk was really something else: terrible temple talk!

If you are a follower of Christ, you are His temple and God's Spirit dwells within you. *Yes, you!* Paul's talking individually, specifically, to me, to you. You there in the yoga pants and flip flops—he means you. And me, and all the saints in Corinth and Ephesus and Grand Rapids and Austin—all of us.

Whether you *feel* like a temple or not, this is the capital "T" Truth. In Christ, when you ask for forgiveness, you become a clean, pure temple—no matter what impure, unimaginable things you've done before. Because of Jesus' death on the cross and His mighty resurrection, we can unpeel those old, ratty sticky labels from our past and replace them with new labels of truth.

 ## Apply It

Write out 1 Corinthians 6:19b–20 (our Chapter 4 memory verse).

How are you doing at *knowing*, *living*, and *sharing* this truth? Are you living like the beautiful, sacred temple that you are? Would you behave differently if you truly believed that the Holy Spirit has permanently moved into your life? How is *your* temple talk?

If you wrestle with terrible temple talk, please know you are not alone. And the good news: we have the mind of Christ (1 Corinthians

2:16). It's time we rip down those lies that have been trashing our thoughts and re-wallpaper our temple with truth![11]

One of the most helpful exercises for me to not only *erase* my old labels but *replace* them with truth was to reflect on the truth of who God says I am—from A to Z.

 Use an NIV Bible and look up the following verses to remind yourself who God says you are. (Perhaps divide the list and accomplish a few letters each day. Don't worry about looking up all twenty-six today.)

A – Romans 15:7

B – Psalm 45:11

C – 1 Peter 2:9a

D – Psalm 116:8

E – 2 Timothy 3:17

F – Galatians 5:1

G – Romans 12:6

H – Ephesians 1:4

I – Romans 6:13

J – Romans 5:1

K – 1 Corinthians 8:3

L – Ephesians 5:8b–9

M – Romans 8:37

N – 2 Corinthians 5:17

O – 1 John 5:4–5

P – John 14:27a

Q – Colossians 1:12

R – Ephesians 1:7

S – Ephesians 4:30

T – 1 Corinthians 6:19a

U – Romans 6:5

V – 1 Corinthians 15:57

W – Ephesians 2:10

X – 1 John 3:1

Y – Matthew 11:29–30

Z – Romans 12:11

Close in prayer, asking God to give you brand-new T³—Truth-filled Temple Talk.

God, we praise You for who You are—good, faithful, loving, and true. Forgive us for the many times we complain, criticize, fuss, and fret about our temple. Please remove the old labels and lies that have been holding us back from experiencing Your fullness and freedom. Renew our mind with Your life-changing Word! Empower us so that we may know, live, and share Your truth with others. In Jesus' name. Amen.

You'll find a completed A to Z list at www.cindybultema.com.

PART FIVE:
Trash & Treasures

> **Memory Verse:** You are not your own; you were bought at a price. Therefore honor God with your bodies.
>
> —1 Corinthians 6:19b–20

From the time my husband John was a young teenager, he dreamed of owning a white Ford Thunderbird Super Coupe with all the bells and whistles. (Don't ask me what those bells and whistles were, by the way.) He focused on that goal with laser intensity, getting up early to deliver newspapers, and later, working all the hours he could get in retail. John saved every penny, waiting for the day he could buy the Thunderbird of his dreams. Then, after ten years of saving, he was able to go to the dealership and buy the car—in cash. No financing, no car payments—that creamy white classic with tan leather interior was finally his!

Naturally, John took meticulous care of his treasure. That car meant everything to him because he had worked tirelessly for it.

And then he met me—and my kid. Jake was a tyke at the time, but he was old enough to be playing soccer and hockey. John and I were falling in love, and I had a sense we would soon be a family.

With a family car. (Do you know where I am going with this story?)

One day my car broke down and was being serviced in a shop. I needed a loaner.

So, my little family—Jake and I—borrowed the Thunderbird and treated it pretty much like a family car. Jake ate a bagel with cream cheese in the back seat and got it all over the place. I had a leaky coffee cup sitting on the console. Little clods of dirt from Jake's soccer cleats became imbedded in the carpet.

Meanwhile, I don't believe my future husband had ever partaken of a single water bottle in his Thunderbird.

I was a mom who turned his Thunderbird into a mom car. His treasure didn't mean nearly as much to me. I didn't sacrifice or slave for its purchase. In my obliviousness, I trashed the car a little bit.

If you're wondering, John was great about it. He never scolded me or Jake, or said much about the way we had treated the Thunderbird. One day though, I opened the door and saw fruit snack wrappers on the floor, and when I sat down, the floor felt sticky to my feet. I felt convicted. I apologized to John, and he graciously forgave me. Then we got married and bought a minivan. The End.

Digging Deeper

It may be the end to that little chapter of my story, but it reminds me of a two-thousand-year-old story, of our friends the Corinthian church members and how they acted obliviously toward the sacred treasure that was their bodies. As we've discovered, they were trashing their bodies like I trashed John's car. Instead of regarding their bodies as treasures, some were sleeping with prostitutes, getting drunk, and gorging themselves on rich food. Their city's lifestyle was pure decadence: self-indulgent, excessive, and depraved.

There are many different ways to abuse one's body.

"Well," we might be thinking, "that's disgusting! Those church members deserve to be royally told off for their bad behavior! Who would ever disregard their bodies like them? Who?"

Well, us today, for starters. There are many different ways to abuse one's body. Just because one is not sleeping with prostitutes doesn't mean one is honoring one's God-given frame.

 What are other ways women in our culture today dishonor their God-given bodies?

 Turn to the familiar words of 1 Corinthians 6:19–20 and summarize them below.

Paul's tone was fatherly, pastoral, kind but firm. Like John's grace toward me after I treated his longed-for Thunderbird like a junk car, Paul exhibited mercy to his brothers and sisters, reminding them of their incalculable worth.

Once more, Paul spoke straight into their specific community—what was common, routine; what they knew in their everyday life. Writers are always told to "write what you know," and again Paul wrote what he knew from living in Corinth for eighteen months. And his letter's addressees would have known exactly what he was talking about: the purchase of slaves.

You are not your own. Paul used slave language here, in a city whose population some scholars estimate was two-thirds slaves.[12] The Greek slaves, of course, belonged to their master, who could dispose of them as he saw fit. He could give them away, sell them, or rent them out at any time. They were considered possessions, human "stuff."

You were bought with a price. Slaves were bought at an auction, like cattle. Most belonged to their master until they died, but they did have a very unique option I learned about while in Greece: They could save their money and buy back their freedom, sometimes taking nearly thirty years to do so. The total amount due would be a slave's street value at that time.

So let's say you were a Greek slave named Daphne who wanted nothing more than to win your freedom from a possibly hard and even abusive master. You would scrape and slave—literally—pinching your "pennies" and saving a few copper coins from your earnings to take to the temple, which also functioned as a kind of bank. It would take weeks, months, even years until one glorious day you realized you had enough to set yourself free. (Well, free-*ish*. I'll explain in a minute.)

The temple priest would preside over the transaction whereby the master would be paid his slave's street value, and the business deal would be formalized in stone. Just as we would sign papers to formalize, say, the buying or selling of a house, the process involved a contract chiseled in a large, flat stone. They would say something like this:

"Daphne is no longer a slave. Daphne has been set free from her master."

When John and I toured the popular archaeological site of Delphi (the religious center of ancient Greece), our tour guide showed us some of these ancient rock contracts, officially called manumission inscriptions. We climbed the stone-paved footpath past remains of columns, pedestals, and small buildings, or treasuries, in which the early Greeks deposited their gifts to the gods. And there on the age-old stone wall, freed slaves carved their names to register their liberation. It was an emotional moment for me—to see concrete evidence of name after name of men and women who had personally inscribed their glorious news of freedom.

Except—and now we get to the "free-ish" part—if you were Daphne, you would now belong to the temple. Daphne no longer had any ties to her old master, but she now had a new master. Was she free? Not really.

We do that, too, don't we? Let's say we're a smoker, and we decide, once and for all, it's time to quit. We spend tons of time and money to stop our smoking habit—we are not going to be a slave to cigarettes any longer. But in place of smoking, we end up snacking on chocolate bars, ice cream, crunchy tortilla chips, and anything else we can devour so we don't think about cigarettes. Have we experienced true freedom? Not really. We just have a new master.

 Can you relate? Have you ever switched from one master to another?

Back to Corinth and Daphne, and you and me and liberation stones. Paul is telling every believer we are not our own. We've been bought with a price. This time, the price was not a slave's thirty years-worth of sacrifice and savings.

 What is the price Paul is talking about here? **Turn to 1 Peter 1:18– 19** and fill in the blanks below.

"For you know it was not with perishable things like silver or gold you were redeemed from the empty way of life . . . but with _____ _____ _____ ___ _____*."*

Christ bought his followers—body, soul, and spirit—through the price of his own death. The very blood of Jesus purchased us from a lifetime of slavery! Can I get an amen?!

In Christ, the sale is complete. We now belong to God—we are members of his family, and our bodies are members of Christ Himself (1 Corinthians 6:15). We've been bought at tremendous cost, and we didn't have to save our coins month after month, year after year. The deal has been chiseled—into a Living Stone, engraved into the hands of our new Master.

Here is the best news of all! Our new Master is not a temple priest, sinful substitute choice, or a "hole-filler"—like cigarettes, tortilla chips, or cookie dough ice cream. Instead, even though we *were* slaves of sin, we now belong to the one true God!

 Listen to a similar message Paul shared while writing from Corinth to the church in Rome. **Look up Romans 6:16–23** and recap Paul's thoughts below.

What amazing promises! We've been completely set free from sin—it is no longer our master! No matter how long or how often we listened to the lies of the enemy or participated in his shady schemes, when we come to Christ—we are *free*! Plus, we've been infused with a divine Helper to empower us to live out our new-found freedom.

 Peek back at 1 Corinthians 6:19 and record who now resides in our treasured temple?

Friend, if Christ is your Master, you have the Holy Spirit living inside of you—in position and prepared to help you live a sparkling-clean life in our sin-saturated world!

Therefore honor God with your body. Because this mind-blowing purchase results in being identified with God, Paul pleaded with the Corinthian believers (and you and me) to obey Christ—fully, eagerly, and thankfully. The Message paraphrases Paul's words this way:

> *Didn't you realize that your body is a sacred place, the place of the Holy Spirit? Don't you see that you can't live however you please, squandering what God paid such a high price for? The physical part of you is not some*

piece of property belonging to the spiritual part of you. God owns the whole works. So let people see God in and through your body.

Yes we are free, but *not* free to satisfy our lusts and cravings as the Corinthians mistakenly thought, returning to their old master: sin. No! Instead, now we are free to *not* sin—to choose to *not* use our bodies any way we want to. We get to make a different choice. This time, we are free to glorify and honor God with our body.

> *We are free to glorify and honor God with our body.*

Paul's two-thousand-year-old emancipation declaration is for us, too. No longer is sin our master. No longer are the world's standards the boss of us. We don't have to earn a high salary, write more blog posts, or save the whales. The world tells us to do these things to earn our worth. But we were bought with a high price.

"[Your name] is no longer a slave to sin. She has been set free from her old master, and now has a new Master. His name is Jesus."

Apply It

Let's start thinking about our bodies—God's sacred temples—in a whole new way. They are more precious and costly than the most awe-inspiring mansion splashed on the pages of *Architectural Digest*. Our bodies are sacred, good, and holy. They have infinite value, and God is incredibly interested in what we do with them.

 What does it look like to treasure your body? What are ways you have trashed it? Fill out the chart on the next page with at least five insights in each column. I'll go first to get us started.

WAYS TO TREASURE THE TEMPLE	WAYS TO TRASH THE TEMPLE
Get plenty of rest	*Ignore my body's need for sleep*

What is one practical action step you can accomplish toward living as God's treasured temple?

Please know, I'm not suggesting you go on a diet, get Botox, or join a fitness Bootcamp. I am suggesting we all reflect on how best to treat our sacred temple, and to pray what we might need to change from this day forward—no matter what we have done in the past.

Back to the manumission inscriptions from Delphi. When I asked our Greek guide about the slave names and why they were inscribed in stone, he replied, "If a slave's freed status was ever questioned, the slave could go to the stone wall and point to his/her name and say: 'See! I have been set free!'"

Pick a stone and write your name and today's date on the "freedom wall" below. Although our *Live Full, Walk Free* wall looks much different than the ancient stone wall of manumission inscriptions in Delphi—let's use our sanctified imaginations and remind ourselves of the magnificent purchase that took place on our behalf!

The next time the enemy tries one of his sneaky lies, or you feel your flesh calling out to trash your sacred temple, point to this page and declare—

I am no longer a slave to sin.

I have been bought at a price.

I have a new Master.

His name is Jesus.

Video Lesson Four:
SEX IN THE SINFUL CITY

Use the space below to note anything that stands out to you from the video lesson. You may also choose to take notes on a separate sheet of paper.

Use the following questions as a guide for group discussion:

1. What stood out to you in today's video teaching? Any new insights?

2. How was the culture of the city of Corinth impacting the Corinthian church members? Do you see the same thing taking place in our churches today? If so, how?

3. Review 1 Corinthians 6:12–20. How might one "flee" sexual immorality in our sex-crazed society (v. 18)? What truth-filled counsel would you share with a sister caught on the hook of sexual sin?

4. Cindy shared, "The road to sin begins in our thought life." Have you found this to be true? What is your current greatest area of temptation? How might *knowing* and *living* 1 Corinthians 10:13 help you on your *live-full-walk-free* journey?

5. Make a #Truth bumper sticker you'd place on your "Corinthian chariot." Ideas include a treasured verse, lyrics to a favorite hymn, or "Know the Truth. Live the Truth. Share the Truth."

CHAPTER FIVE

To Eat or Not to Eat

Prayer:

O God, thank You that You are for me. How amazing to think that the God of all creation knows me, enjoys me, and longs to have an intimate relationship with me. Forgive me for the times I get busy, distracted, and/or enticed by the enemy and his schemes. I want to know You more. Teach me, guide me, show me how powerful and mighty You are. Lord, how I desire to be used by You to show others Your truth, love, and grace. Remind me that love is like a magnet that will draw others to You. May I sprinkle Your love and kindness everywhere I go so that others might experience your fullness and freedom. In the redeeming name of Jesus I pray. Amen.

PART ONE:
Q & A with Pastor Paul

> **Memory Verse:** Be careful, however, that the exercise of your rights does not become a stumbling block to the weak.
>
> —1 Corinthians 8:9

After twenty-six years of living my own way, surrendering my life to Jesus was wonderful—but it also raised many, many questions.

I mean, I was clueless about so much stuff. It was like I had lived over a quarter of a century on another planet, and now I had to learn all the customs of life on my new planet. I wondered . . .

❧ What do you say when you pray? Do you just start babbling? Do you open or shut your eyes?

❧ How much money should I give to my church? Was it responsible of me to give when I was a single mom in oodles of debt?

❧ How do I begin to teach my little boy about God when I know so little? (Thank goodness for *Veggie Tales*! Jake is twenty-two and still has "God Is Bigger Than the Boogie Man" stuck in his head!)

The Corinthian Christians were in a similar spot. After years of living in morally polluted Corinth, they also had loads of questions about how to *live full* and *walk free* as new believers.

 Record Paul's opening words in **1 Corinthians 7**.

Chapter 7 introduces a new section, a kind of "FAQs about Life in Sin City." After addressing the reports of their infighting and moral lapses, Paul changed gears to answer some of *their* questions. It was time for Q and A with Pastor Paul!

 What were your first questions when you became a believer? What would you ask Pastor Paul if you could?

Digging Deeper

As we've learned, Corinth was messed up to begin with, and the murky, muddled institution of marriage just added to the disorder. In the first-century Greco-Roman world, your marriage would have been arranged by your family.

> *Don't like the idea that Ajax the sail maker has fish breath and a hairy back? Tough. He's going to be your husband anyway, if that's the match your parents made for you.*
>
> *Have a problem with the age difference between you and Aquila and the fact that he has the personality of a squid? Too bad, so sad. The wedding's on Tuesday at 4 p.m.*

So, you were probably married to someone you did not love, never mind the complexities that would have followed. In Corinth, it was normal for a husband and wife to sleep in separate bedrooms. Your husband's mistress(es) would have been part of your household too. (Corinth was way ahead of TLC's "Sister Wives"!) The maxim about marriage was this: You have wives to produce children, mistresses for company, and prostitutes for sexual pleasure.

But wait—it gets worse! Some church members had misinterpreted Paul's earlier message about abstaining from sexual immorality and now believed all sex was sinful, therefore Christians shouldn't get married. Others were saying married Christians should be celibate. Thankfully, they wrote to Paul to help set their twisted thinking straight.

 Read 1 Corinthians 7:1–16. What stands out to you from Paul's marriage message? Any surprises?

Paul wasn't bashful about discussing the subject of sex, singleness, marriage, and divorce in a sincere and straightforward manner! But let's be careful not to misunderstand Paul's position. Yes, he answered that an unmarried, sex-free life is good, but he was not saying that singleness is a suitable lifestyle for everyone. In fact, due to the countless number of sexual temptations in Sin City, Paul recommended marrying rather than to "burn with passion." He considered both marriage and singleness to be gifts from God.

 Read 1 Corinthians 7:17 and then write it out below.

I love how The Message puts it:

And don't be wishing you were someplace else or with someone else. Where you are right now is God's place for you. *Live and obey and love and believe right there. God, not your marital status, defines your life. Don't think I'm being harder on you than on the others. I give this same counsel in all the churches* (emphasis added).

Paul was saying, "Listen, you guys have been through a huge life-altering change by choosing Christ. Now is not the time to make major changes in your life. Stay put and don't add to the mess and chaos by changing your job, your wife, your marital status."

Just a few verses later, he reinforced this thought:

Each person should remain in the situation they were in when God called them (v. 20).

And he said it again in verse 24:

Brothers and sisters, each person, as responsible to God, should remain in the situation they were in when God called them.

Three times in short order, Paul charged the brothers and sisters to remain where they were in life. Stay. Abide. Stand. This counsel must have seemed counterintuitive to them. Their lives had changed radically, so why wouldn't they make radical changes to their life situations? Why wouldn't a Christian married to a pagan wonder if she should leave him? Why wouldn't a slave wonder if she were now to be free physically as well as spiritually?

I remember a time when my life changed radically—and not for the better. In 1998, I was engaged to be married, when my fiancé David was killed in a freak workplace accident. I loved David deeply and didn't know if I would ever heal. We had planned to build a Christian home and grow old together. I had a gorgeous white wedding dress bought and laid aside for my wedding, five months later. But on that unthinkable day, two weeks before Christmas, I got the call that sent a wrecking ball through my life.[1]

My life changed in one horrific moment, and suddenly I wanted to change everything. Everything felt so wrong. I couldn't control David's premature death, but I could control my actions. I could change jobs and routines and even my furniture. I had this intense impulse to change everything! But the counterintuitive wisdom on grieving teaches something else: the grieving one shouldn't change anything for at least one year. Instead, sit with the pain. Abide. Live where you are and come to terms with your new normal. And learn to be content, even though your heart is shattered.

I think this is what Paul was getting at with the Corinthians: Be content where you are, in the life situation you are in. Paul wasn't saying their social, religious, or marital status was an unchangeable divine appointment, but that their present life should be an avenue for ministry. Don't focus on changing the outside; instead let God change you on the inside.

According to Paul, happiness is not dependent on circumstances.

In those aching days and weeks after David's death, my wise mentor offered me some of the most meaningful words. "You always have a choice, Cindy," she said gently. "You can be better or bitter." I could choose pitiful or powerful. Oh, but it was so hard sometimes. But God helped me choose *better*, and He helped me choose *powerful*. He provided many opportunities to share His comfort with others. He used David's death to bring my dad to Jesus. The pain of my past shaped me into the woman that my husband John fell in love with.

"Where you are right now is God's place for you." Did the Corinthians believe that? Do we?

Let's say you're . . .

- ❀ Twenty-eight and not married. You thought life would turn out so differently: by now you'd have had the perfect, Pinterest-inspired wedding and maybe even an Instagrammable baby shower.

- ❀ Thirty-eight, and your life with three kids is one big chauffeuring job. You might as well paint your car yellow and slap a TAXI sign on it.

- ❀ Forty-eight, and you thought things would be different: your family would be close, your income would be comfortable, and your marriage would be fulfilling. But your teenagers are snarky, you struggle to make ends meet, and your marriage is lackluster on a good day.

It's easy to be discontent with our singleness or our marriage; being frantically busy with little ones or ignored by our teenagers. But according to Paul, happiness is not dependent on circumstances. Most people get caught in "when/then" thinking:

"When I lose weight, then I'll be happy."
"When I get married, then I won't be so lonely."
"When I get the bills paid off, then . . . !"

 Your turn, friend. Fill in the blanks with your most often spoken "when/then" proclamations.

When _____ ,
then _____ .

When _____ ,
then _____ .

When _____ ,
then _____ .

But Paul says *now* is the time. Today. Here and now. In the present.

 Paul knew what he was talking about when it came to finding contentment in *any* circumstance. **Turn to Philippians 4:12** and record a summary of this powerful verse below.

Philippians was the letter Paul wrote to the believers in Philippi, a place he resided on his second missionary journey. He also spent a little time in jail there!

Incredibly, on our trip to Greece, John and I were able to go to Philippi and see the small, rocky structure traditionally identified as Paul and Silas's holding cell. I was struck by how tight those quarters would have been for two grown men. Scholars tell us most cells were dark, especially the inner cells of a prison, like the one Paul and Silas inhabited in Philippi. Excruciating cold, hunger, loneliness, and stomach-turning odors made life behind bars unbearable.

Yet Paul was able to say from prison, "I've learned the secret of being content in any and every situation." Amazing!

Obviously, Paul was more concerned about the *attitudes* of the believers rather than their life situations. He had demonstrated his God-boosted bravery in prison and other hard places, proving a Christ follower doesn't need a change in circumstances to find spiritual contentment.

❧ *Apply It*

Like the Corinthians, we need to make intentional choices to be content in our current circumstances. Now, being content does not necessarily mean being resigned to the fact that you might not get married, get a great job, or retire early. It simply means being willing to let God guide you and work in your life *wherever* you are in your current season.

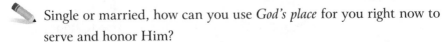 Single or married, how can you use *God's place* for you right now to serve and honor Him?

Write a prayer asking God to forgive you for the times you wished you were given a different assignment. Acknowledge your need for Him, especially if you are wrestling to embrace this season as His place for you. Share with Him your feelings about your current circumstances. Thank Him for the promise that your worth is not based on your marital status, social situation, or any of life's challenges. Invite God to replenish you with His strength to help you *live* and *share* this truth with others.

PART TWO:
Where's the Beef?

> **Memory Verse:** Be careful, however, that the exercise of your rights does not become a stumbling block to the weak.
>
> —1 Corinthians 8:9

I have a friend I'll call Jayne. Jayne joined a book club a few years ago with a bunch of her hockey mom friends, not entirely knowing what she was getting herself into. She was the only Christian in the group, and from the first meeting, when the topic of séances dominated a discussion of a Mary Todd Lincoln biography, Jayne knew she had a calling among those women. Oh, she enjoyed them, and loved laughing with them and sometimes even crying with them when certain books reminded them of their deeper stories (as books often do).

But she felt called to be among them, all the same. She was the one voice of truth in a group that thought Satan was fictional and that a Ouija board was as harmless as playing Scattergories. As she grew in love for her "non-religious" friends, Jayne realized things might get "awkward" as she navigated the book club dynamics. She wasn't always sure when she should speak up in support of her faith or when she should remain quiet. Jayne prayed for wisdom as she read each book, trying to anticipate—but never quite being able to do so—how the monthly discussion would go.

Most often, she was able to read and discuss the book of the month without worrying about it being a bad influence on her. She found books were a great "open door" leading to deeper conversations about life and faith. For Jayne, being *in* the world but not *of* the world meant not jumping into a Christian cave but rather joining in the cultural conversations around her.

One month, however, Jayne was faced with a very "sticky situation." Helen in her group had picked *Fifty Shades of Grey* as the next month's selection. Jayne didn't know much about it, other than it was an erotic book that everyone was talking about. She immediately felt uncomfortable, and wondered if she should skip the next book club. On the one hand, this was THE book everyone was talking about, which was Jayne's thing. On the other hand, the book was famously racy—should a Christ follower be reading it?

Talk about a "gray" area! Jayne prayed for wisdom and received it on social media soon after. A young pastor she trusted posted about how *Fifty Shades of Grey* glamorized sexual perversion and even abuse of women. "Christian women—please don't read this!" he pleaded on Facebook. It was the voice of truth she had prayed for. Jayne was about to email the group and tell them she was opting out—and why—when a fellow member beat her to it and said the "anti-feminist vibe" made her uncomfortable. Jayne still felt led to share her thoughts as graciously as possible, and the group moved on to another book.

Jayne had encountered a "gray area," one of those fuzzy situations that don't seem to offer black or white solutions. "Gray areas are issues that Scripture does not take a dogmatic (strict) stance on, or at the very least, issues that Scripture does not discuss in depth. Instead, the Bible gives Christians the liberty to make God-glorifying decisions based on their convictions," shares Discipleship Defined.[2]

 According to this quote, how can we know if our "sticky situation" is a gray area or black and white?

Many times we'll encounter situations where we *do* know the answer because it is stated in the Bible as truth—a biblical absolute, a spiritual principle. For example, we know the Bible teaches us not to lie, steal, kill, or slander (Exodus 20)—those are spiritual *principles.*

Some might call spiritual principles the "dos and don'ts of the Bible," the "thou shalts and thous shalt nots," clear instructions specifically found in Scripture.

But what does Scripture say about gray areas, such as: who to vote for, which movies to see, what words are acceptable, and how to dress? What about yoga—is it okay? Or a glass of sangria? How many times can we visit the dessert buffet before we veer into glutton territory? Those are spiritual *preferences,* or the gray areas of our Christian walk.

 Can you think of three spiritual principles and three spiritual preferences? Add them to the chart below. (If you can think of a Scripture verse for the spiritual principle, give yourself a gold star.)

SPIRITUAL PRINCIPLES	SPIRITUAL PREFERENCES

Digging Deeper

The Corinthians had countless questions about the gray areas they were now faced with in the midst of their everyday life. Thankfully they *knew the truth* that they were free in Christ, but they were confused about how to *live the truth*, especially when it came to areas not clearly defined in the Bible.

Read 1 Corinthians 8:1–13. Note your initial thoughts and/or questions.

Paul started out chapter 8 responding to a major gray area for the Christ followers in Corinth: "food sacrificed to idols."

I don't know about you, but it's at this point where I'm tempted to skip ahead in my Bible reading plan. I mean, idol meat? Really— what does that have to do with anything we face today? When was the last time you or I waffled over whether or not to chow down on a bacon cheeseburger (well, unless it was about the number of calories or we're vegan)? Never—but that doesn't mean there's not guidance in this passage for us today. Stick with me and Pastor Paul on this one—you'll be glad you did.

First, let's take a look at the actual issue of eating idol meat so we can understand the context. The Christians in Corinth were probably not worshiping idols any longer, so did it matter if they were eating a lamb stew that was sacrificed to one? Yet, it *did* matter very much to some folks, because they felt that eating this meat was being affiliated with or endorsing idol worship.

Let's say a certain fast food chain openly promotes abortion rights. Some of us might have a problem with eating there knowing a portion of our bill might potentially go toward supporting a cause that makes us uncomfortable. Others among us feel differently; we can eat there with a clear conscience because we are pro-life, and besides, we believe that "boycotting" is an ineffective way to engage in cultural conversation.

But, but, but . . . how could they? You might think. How could anyone who is pro-life eat there? Or, you may also think the opposite: How could anyone who cares about making change in our culture *not* eat there—aiming to lovingly treat the restaurant as a mission field, to seek understanding and win hearts for Jesus *and* the pro-life movement?

You see, that's the problem with gray areas. Usually there's little agreement on how to handle them. Even if you know you're right, beyond a shadow of your Corinthian crispy chicken, does it mean that's what's right for your sister or brother, too?

Back to idol meat and the issues it was causing in Corinth. This was a big deal—because if you had a problem with it, the matter was inescapable. Temples were on nearly every corner in town, idolatry was everywhere, and meat sacrificed to idols? Why, our ancient pals would run into this provocative pork as regularly as we run into provocative magazine covers at the corner store.

There were three main sticky occasions where the Corinthians would have encountered idol meat:

1. **Eating in the pagan temples**: The temples in Corinth would have been used as venues to host get-togethers for public affairs or business and social functions. It would have been completely normal to visit a temple for a wedding, work meeting, or another community-wide event. Business dinner at the temple? Better pack some hummus chips if you have a problem with idol meat.

2. **Buying meat in the marketplace**: Even meat that was not openly taken to the pagan temples was often blessed by the merchant as a symbolic offering to an idol. If a Christian purchased

meat in the market, there was always a possibility that it had been offered to an idol.

3. **Eating dinner at the home of friends and neighbors**: When Christians were invited to eat dinner with pagan neighbors, there was no guarantee that the meat they were served had not been sacrificed to an idol.

Of course, our quarrelsome friends in the Corinthian church community were at odds over what certain people ate for dinner. Some Corinthian Christ followers felt they were free to eat whatever they wanted, even meats offered to idols. Let's call them the Liberated Ones. They were so convinced in their liberty that they consumed idol-meats at meals—no problem! They were free in Christ, right?!

Other Corinthian Christians—let's call them the Sensitive Ones—made a much bigger fuss. These brothers and sisters would not have dreamed of taking even a nibble of a lamb chop without knowing the name and serial number of its farmer and the barometric pressure the day it was slaughtered. "Every meal must have been like an inquisition, with the host being grilled (pardon the pun) concerning the origin of the meat being served," writes Bible teacher Bob Deffinbaugh.[3]

Thankfully, Paul established a principle about preferences, a standard for how to deal with gray matters of every kind.

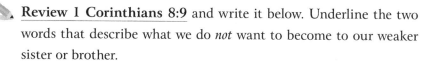 **Review 1 Corinthians 8:9** and write it below. Underline the two words that describe what we do *not* want to become to our weaker sister or brother.

Translation: You might think you are free to (a) eat idol meat, (b) drink sangria, (c) wear a bikini, or (d) read an R-rated book, and maybe you are. You may well be within your rights as a believer to do those things. But don't let being right get in the way of love for someone who, for whatever reason, can't handle your level of freedom.

And do we want to cause someone to stumble in their faith, or struggle in any way? Absolutely not! Have you ever gone flying over a stumbling block—tripping, slipping, staggering in the process. Oh my! It all sounds so painful, and trust me, it is!

> *Don't let being right get in the way of love for someone who can't handle your level of freedom.*

Last year, my family and I were at the airport in Orlando preparing to fly home to Michigan. My youngest daughter and I stopped in at Orange Julius to grab some smoothies for us and my other daughter. With one daughter's smoothie in one hand and mine in the other, I walked briskly back to our gate when suddenly I hit a slippery patch on the floor. I flailed as my feet went out from under me, but somehow—miraculously—I landed on my knees still clenching two smoothies in a death grip.

I didn't think anyone would notice a red-haired, middle-aged woman on her knees in the middle of the terminal, but everyone was staring. And gasping. "Let's keep moving, Mom," said my sweet girl, mortified, as I struggled to get up.

To this day, I'm still not sure how that happened—I'm normally not a klutz. But out of nowhere, I definitely hit a slippery spot and went flying. It can happen to the best of us.

Paul didn't want the more liberated church members to cause their weaker brothers and sisters to take a similar fall. He used the Greek word *proskomma*, which means "an obstacle put in the path which would cause people to stumble if they bump their foot against it, or that over which a soul stumbles, i.e. by which it is caused to sin."[4]

The Message paraphrases Paul's words this way:

God does care when you use your freedom carelessly in a way that leads a fellow believer still vulnerable to those old associations to be thrown off track. —1 Corinthians 8:8–9

In other words, Paul was saying, "Yes, you do have a right. You are free to eat the lamb chop! But, dear sister and brother, you can be right and still be wrong."

When it comes to the gray areas of life—love trumps knowledge.

You may have a clean conscience about who you vote for—you may even be right. But when you start skewering your brother at the Thanksgiving dinner table for his oh-so-wrong political views, you take a wrong turn anyway.

Yes, you have the right to wear tight running shorts and your short workout bra into your favorite coffeehouse. But beautiful sister, when you dress in body-hugging attire, it may be a stumbling block for your male brothers. Be careful.

This is especially vital on social media. We are often puffed up with our own knowledge to the exclusion of our fellow human beings, God's image bearers. Love considers and thinks things through. Love leans in and listens, setting aside our rights and freedoms.

Knowledge alone says, "I have a right to do what I want. I know I'm right!" But Knowledge + Love says, "How will my choices affect my sisters and brothers? My life is not just about me."

Apply It

How have you been impacted by spiritual preferences? Can you think of a situation where you, like Jayne, were faced with a gray area?

✏️ Circle any gray areas you've encountered below. (If you think any activity on the list is a spiritual principle, not a spiritual preference, cross it out.)

Dancing	Kissing	Working out- side the home
Movies	Spending of money	Yoga
Gambling	Halloween	Smoking
Clothing	TV	Birth control
Music	Homeschooling	Language/swearing
Alcohol		

Other:

✏️ Thinking back over your experiences, do you tend to give people grace in gray areas? Explain.

✏️ Can you remember a time where you were *not* given grace in a gray area? How did/does it make you feel?

✏️ Invite God to bring to mind any situations where being right has become more important than being loving, or gray areas where you need to remember: love trumps knowledge.

PART THREE:
Margaritas, Meat, & Messes

Memory Verse: Be careful, however, that the exercise of your rights does not become a stumbling block to the weak.

—1 Corinthians 8:9

I'll never forget the summer I had a chaotic house filled with two babies, one toddler, a travel-hockey-playing son—plus John, who was working a brand new, stress-filled job. My mind was mushy after reading *Dora the Explorer* and *Thomas the Tank Engine* books day and night; not to mention lugging hockey goalie gear from one cold ice rink to another every weekend. I was desperate for some girlfriend time! Imagine my delight when some of my friends invited me for a girls night out. Yes, please!

Now for most Christian women, this wouldn't lead to a sticky situation—but for me, sadly, it did.

You know by now of my former addiction to alcohol and drugs, and how I became clean and sober at the age of twenty-six by the power of Jesus Christ. Over the past twenty years I have been able to *live full* and *walk free* in these addictive areas (thank You, Jesus), but I still need to be wise about my choices and environments.

So when these friends—all of them Christians—invited me for a "GNO," complete with margaritas on the patio of a favorite restaurant, it sounded enjoyable . . . but scary. Was this a good idea? Could I handle a margarita or two? I have to say, my friends were not taking no for an answer. "Why shouldn't a Bible teacher be able to go out and have fun? One cocktail won't kill you," they coaxed. "C'mon, Cindy—we'll have a great time!" I don't know if they were trying to pressure me, but I felt it. Ultimately I caved, thinking

"What's the big whoop? They're right. I'm making a big deal out of nothing."

So one warm summer night soon after, I took off my mom jeans, put on some cute capris and sparkly lipstick, and joined the get-together. I drank two margaritas, and my friends were right—they didn't kill me. I had a "great" time—although throughout the evening of laughs I felt a growing sense of concern that I had made a poor choice.

Can I be real? I wrestled all summer long with a strong thirst for alcohol after that gathering. Suddenly, it was much harder to say no than it had been in a long time. I felt just like the 1 Corinthians 8 "weaker sister." Going out for margaritas with the girls was a stumbling block on my journey—a major stumbling block.

 Can you think of an example in your own life where you have been impacted by a "stumbling block"? (Peek back at yesterday's lesson for a stumbling block definition, if needed.)

Yesterday, I told the story of wiping out in an airport. Suddenly coming upon a slippery spot on the terminal floor caused me to lose my footing in a very public fashion.

Spiritually speaking, I did something similar when I went out with my "stronger sisters," because surely they were the stronger ones in regard to having a drink on a summer's evening. Yet personally, I slipped in my self-control and strength, and ended up struggling for a season.

In **1 Corinthians 8:9**, Paul talks about things that make us trip and fall. Fill in the blanks to our memory verse below.

"_____ _____ , *however, that the exercise of your* _____ *does* _____ *become a* _____ _____*to the* _____*.*"

My girlfriends were well within their rights to have a drink. No judgment here! None of them became drunk, which is what the Bible commands us not to do.[5] This was not a gray area at all for them, just a simple choice—crushed ice or on the rocks. For me, with my past history and weakness to addiction, this sticky situation was umpteen shades of gray. Unintentionally, my friends had put their freedoms above my weak spot. The result—a "block" was thrown in my path and I stumbled and nearly fell, which is why I now meet all of my friends for coffee.

For our Corinthian sisters, the gray area was not margaritas, yoga pants, Harry Potter, or watching something racy on Netflix. You could say for them it was all about the beef, or more to the point, beef and other meats which had been sacrificed to idols.

A recap of the idol-meat issue: Some Corinthian believers, especially those with a background of idol worship, still found the issue very sticky. Because idol worship had been a part of their past, they wanted nothing to do with it in their present—whether idols were real or not. Other church members had no problem whatsoever with eating sacrificed meat, believing that idols were merely hunks of wood or stone; therefore the meat was *not* defiled or tainted.

To illustrate, imagine two first-century Christians named Wanda and Sally. Both are former idolaters, now saved by grace. Wanda recoils from everything to do with her old way of life, including the meat sold in the marketplace, because for her, eating such meat would be way too close to coming back to her old life. Sally says no to the pagan festivals, but she has no problem eating meat if she's at a dinner party with friends.

Wanda understands that an idol cannot contaminate a good Apollo burger—but she still doesn't feel right eating one. Then one day, Wanda sees Sally eating idol meat. "What? How can that be?' Wanda is completely shocked, but Sally makes light of it and urges her to try some. When Wanda balks, Sally tells her she's being silly and stuck in her ways. "You're free, remember?" Sally mutters. Feeling shamed and pressured, Wanda takes a little morsel of the meat and soon feels sick. Her evening is ruined, and so, maybe, is her friendship with Sally.

 Who was wrong and who was right in this illustration? Can you relate more with the "weaker sister" Wanda or the "stronger sister" Sally? How so?

❧ Digging Deeper

This fictional story is exactly what was taking place in the Corinthian church. The discussion of idol meat and who was right was causing major confusion, clashes, and fallouts! Thus the reason the Christ followers sent Paul a letter asking, "Paul, who is right? Can we eat the meat, or not?" Each one thinking, of course, they were precisely right and their confused brother and sister was oh so wrong!

Before we look at Paul's response, peek back at pages 182–183 and review the three main sticky occasions where the Corinthians would have encountered idol meat.

While John and I toured the ruins of Corinth, we realized how easy it would have been for leftover idol meat to make its way from one of the pagan temples to a nearby market. As we stood in the dusty agora, or market square, our Greek guide pointed out the ruins of many archaic temples: Apollo, Aphrodite, Hera, and Octavia, to name just a few. He explained how two general markets hugged the wall of one great temple, and a fish and meat market was located just across a narrow street from another. Amazingly, all of this was within 150 yards of the center of town. It'd be trouble-free for the temple priests to transport the unused beef, pork, or lamb to a nearby marketplace for purchase.[6]

Not to mention, during the pagan festival times, the price of meat would be significantly reduced to next-to-nothing prices. (Remember, there were no refrigerators. Lots of extra meat amounted to extremely low prices.) If you were a poorer person in Corinth, your only opportunity to purchase meat all year long might be from buying discounted idol meat.

Are you curious to how Paul would bring clarity to this complicated state of affairs? Was it right or wrong for the Christians in Corinth to eat idol meat? Could they fire up the grill or should they stick with their homegrown olives and fresh-baked flatbread?

 Read the following Scripture passages. Summarize Paul's wise counsel about how to respond to idol meat and write it the chart below.

CONTEXT	SCRIPTURE PASSAGE	PAUL'S GUIDANCE
Eating in the pagan temples	1 Corinthians 8:9–13	
Buying meat in the marketplace	1 Corinthians 10:23–25	
Eating dinner at the home of friends and neighbors	1 Corinthians 10:27–33	

I love how Paul handled this sticky situation. He recognized the issue of idol meat had the potential to split the church and cause even greater conflict in Corinth. Instead of directly answering their question, he took a step back and reminded them of the importance of considering the context. In other words, review each unique situation carefully and prayerfully. What might be "right" with one group of friends may be very "wrong" with another.

"Paul, can I eat the meat? Just tell me—yes or no?"

"It depends," replied the patient pastor. "Yes, you are right; you are free to eat the meat. But—you can be right, and still be wrong. Love trumps knowledge."

How do we apply Paul's idol meat guidance to our lives today as we navigate gray areas, such as watching the latest movie, reading the bestselling book, or drinking the cocktail at GNO? Here are four questions that might be helpful to consider:

1. *What does the Bible say about this issue?*

Let's make sure this is a gray area and not a black and white one. Double check: is this a spiritual *principle* found in God's Word or a spiritual *preference*?

Let's say someone shares some juicy gossip at the girls' volleyball game about the new coach and her lousy decisions. There's no need for uncertainty about what to do. If you're tempted to join in on the backbiting talkfest and ramble on about why you think she stinks too—stop.

Gossip is not gray. (See Leviticus 19:16 and James 1:26 for a reminder.)

On the other hand, don't make your spiritual *preferences* another person's spiritual *principles*. When it comes to alcohol, the Bible is explicit about not "falling into drunkenness," but it doesn't say "Thou Shalt Not Have a Beer at the Ball Game." Our preference may be that no one drinks, but we can't make our preferences into principles. Just because we don't approve of something doesn't make it unbiblical.

2. *What is loving?*

Reread 1 Corinthians 8:1 and fill in the blanks below.

"But knowledge _____ up, while _____

_____ _____._"

Oh my—the last thing we want to do is be puffy! Many of the gray areas we wrestle with are matters of personal preference. As different believers, we come at the same issues from various angles, perspectives, and backgrounds.

Love *always* leads us to consider how our choices will impact others. How will our "right" actions affect others who are watching our example? Love always guides us to choices that *build up* our sisters and brothers.

Perhaps we disagree with a post on Facebook (and we *will* disagree with posts on Facebook). How might we disagree in a loving manner? Even if we *know* we are right, would it be loving to "go after" the person who posted, leaving snarky comments stating all the reasons they are wrong and we are right? Love pulls up a chair—privately—and says, "Tell me your thoughts on this matter. You matter. Your opinion matters. I'd love to share a conversation."

3. *What is helpful?*

Review 1 Corinthians 10:23–24. The believers in Corinth may have felt like they "have the right to do anything," but how did Paul respond to their false beliefs? He gently reminded them in verse 23:

"But not everything is _____ or

_____._"

In Wanda and Sally's case, it wasn't helpful for Sally to make light of her friend's sensitivities about idol meat. She may have been "right," but her actions were distinctly unhelpful. We may have the right to read a certain book, watch a certain Netflix series, or listen to certain love songs on the radio, but will doing so be beneficial for us—and our neighbors?

 Can you think of anything in your life that you have the "right to do," but it would not be helpful to participate in?

4. *What will build up the body of Christ?*

 I appreciate Paul's truth-filled words in **1 Corinthians 10:31–33**. Summarize them below:

Love for our sisters and brothers in Christ should guide and help keep in check our freedom in Christ. Our first concern should not be to apply our liberty to the limit—"I'm free! So who cares!"—but to genuinely think about the well-being of our church family.

If my preference—whether it's to eat calorie-laden cheesecake, watch a profanity-filled movie, or overspend on a girls shopping trip—leads you to violate your conscience, then I will cheerfully give up that right when I am with you.

Our sisters and brothers must matter more than our (fill in the blank with your favorite gray area). Let's be mindful of how our choices can help build the beautiful, sacred temple of Christ.

The next time when we are faced with a gray areas—that's *when*, not *if*—may we be gracious to one another. Kind. Helpful. Full of grace and understanding. Ultimately, we are a family, and family takes care of one another.

 *Apply It*

 Peek back at your list of gray areas from yesterday's lesson. Write below any gray areas that are currently impacting you.

 How might the four questions from today's lesson help you make the best decision when faced with a spiritual preference? Rewrite them below and then use them as a guide as you consider—prayerfully and carefully—how to navigate the gray areas of life.

PART FOUR:
Run, Girlfriend, Run!

> **Memory Verse:** Be careful, however, that the exercise of your rights does not become a stumbling block to the weak.
>
> —1 Corinthians 8:9

My eighth-grade son, Benj, is playing junior varsity hockey at the high school this year. Twice a week he gets up at 5:30 a.m. to join his team at the school weight room. Then, he has two ice practices a week after school, plus conditioning that involves running, jumping on boxes, and other taxing activities. Sometimes the training makes Benj vomit—it's that intense. *He's fourteen, people!*

But does Benj quit? No way! Benj is on a mission to mature as an athlete, and he aspires to be in top-notch shape. He knows the importance of faithful, daily training if he's going to help his team triumph. He even started running in the early morning darkness on his "off" days—at which point Mama Bear here stepped in and called *Too Much*.

Don't get me wrong, this hockey mom wants the sweet smell of victory for both her boys and their teams. But I sometimes wonder—what is the reward for all of this crazy-hard work? To which Benj replies, "Mom, without training there will be no reward." Good point, son. Good point!

Training offers important life lessons, not just on the ice rink but ones that can help us *live full* and *walk free*.

Let's lace up our running shoes (metaphorically, that is), and delve deep in Paul's famous "run the race" analogy.

Read 1 Corinthians 9:24–27, and write out verse 24:

Digging Deeper

Paul was partial to switching out his metaphors, and as before (think under rowers and temples) this one was spot on for his audience. The Corinthians loved athletics! They sponsored the biannual Isthmian Games, a sporting event held right outside their city, second in size only to the Olympics. John and I toured the Isthmia Archaeological Site, trekking past the ruins of Poseidon's temple, the timeworn city wall rubble, and even the Games' ancient starting block—complete with an elaborate system of strings which allowed the athletes to start instantaneously.

Our tour leader, Professor Franz, taught us that the competition included foot races, wrestling, boxing, throwing the discus and javelin, the long jump, chariot racing, poetry reading, and singing. (I'm guessing poetry would have been my best shot at entering.)

And get this: Women *did* enter the games! In the Isthmia Museum, we found several age-old inscriptions naming the women who won the 200-meter dash as well as the war-chariot races. How cool!

Can you guess the most popular event in the Isthmian Games?

If you guessed chariot racing—guess again. Foot races were all the rage at the Isthmian Games. So when Paul described a runner in the Christian life, the Corinthians would have had a vivid mental image.

"Run in such a way . . ."

The word *run* in the Greek is *trecho*, which means "to exert one's self, strive hard; to spend one's strength in performing or attaining something."[7]

The Corinthians could visualize the preparation needed to compete successfully: the months of focused training, the single-minded dedication, the essential running pace, plus some old-fashioned blood, sweat, and tears!

So Paul was telling the Christ followers, "Don't walk. Don't stop. Don't sit down. Give the Christian life your all! *Run!*"

The same encouragement is intended for you and me too—*run!* God did not set you apart to have you sit in the stands. He didn't call you to tiptoe alongside the track. God has not empowered you with *dunamis* power to stand by the sidelines watching and waiting while everyone else runs. Girlfriend, *you* have a race to run. Yes, *you*! *Run!*

"*. . . as to take the prize.*"

Let's be clear: Paul wasn't referring to the actual prize won by the top Isthmian Games athletes. Because they didn't win a gold medal, or even silver or bronze. Nope. You know what you won in the Isthmian Games?

Celery.

Yes, celery.

No shiny gold medal looped around your neck. No studio full of glamorous prizes. No endorsement deals for protein bars or teeth whitening strips or vitamins.

After ten months of nonstop single-minded training, the prize for the fastest runner was a crown of crunchy green vegetation. Well, maybe it wasn't even so crunchy by the time it made it to your head. Our Greek guide said by the time you received your celery wreath, it was already wilted. No wonder Paul referred to this prize as "perishable" in some translations—literally it would have shriveled up and rotted within days of receiving it.

So, if it's not celery, what prize was Paul actually talking about here?

The Greek word is *stephanos,* or crown. Paul used the same word among the final ones he penned to Timothy. Circle the word *crown* in the passage below.

> *I have fought the good and worthy and noble fight, I have finished the race, I have kept the faith [firmly guarding the gospel against error]. In the future there is reserved for me the [victor's] crown of righteousness [for being right with God and doing right], which the Lord, the righteous Judge, will award to me on that [great] day—and not to me only, but also to all those who have loved and longed for and welcomed His appearing.*
> —2 Timothy 4:7–8 AMP

 Who else does Paul say will receive a crown when they finish their race?

This is the mind-boggling grace of God! We receive the joy of *living full* and *walking free* here on earth; and in addition, God blesses us with earthly and heavenly rewards for serving him devotedly. What a great, great God!

So if you and I have a race to run and an imperishable prize to attain, how do we get into peak-performance condition? What do we need to do to prepare?

 Pastor Paul clarified in **1 Corinthians 9:25**. Write it out below:

The strenuous training of an Isthmian Games competitor lasted ten months. Each medal-hopeful contender would need to say no to perfectly permissible behaviors and activities, and/or any hindrances to their game-day performance. And for athletes living in "anything goes" Corinth, the temptations were everywhere and anywhere! *But*

runners needed to stay focused and exhibit self-control. They were in strict training!

Similarly, Paul was saying that following Christ may be demanding and strenuous. Our faith race will take hard work, perseverance, and discipline. It also requires intense spiritual vigilance. We can't be "out of shape" and expect to live a set-apart, holy life any more than a Corinthian could expect to walk into a stadium without having prepared and secure a first place victory.

Instead of *trying* to live a holy life, we need to *train* in holiness. No one can make us, and no one can do it for us. Training isn't easy, but the reward will be oh so worth it. Run in such a way as to get the prize! Let's exercise discipline and self-control so we can cross that finish line triumphantly!

Apply It

I love Paul's personal gusto and zeal captured in The Message paraphrase of 1 Corinthians 9:26–27:

> *I don't know about you, but I'm running hard for the finish line. I'm giving it everything I've got. No sloppy living for me! I'm staying alert and in top condition. I'm not going to get caught napping, telling everyone else all about it and then missing out myself.*

 How about you, friend? Are you running purposefully for the finish line of your faith? Would you describe your faith journey as one of mostly *training* or mainly *trying*?

Following are three training tips to help us get rid of sloppy living, and get ready for our race!

❀ *Define your race.*

What race are you running? What do you desire to do with your one and only life? Our task is to find the plans and purposes God has for our lives, and then avidly run *that* race.

John Piper says in his book *Don't Waste Your Life*, "Desire that your life count for something great! Long for your life to have eternal significance. Want this! Don't coast through life without a passion."[8]

How would you define your race? Peek at your calendar, email inbox, and check book. Where are you investing your time, talent, energies and effort?

Describe your race in the box below. Write down words that communicate your life mission and vision, values and purpose.

[box]

❀ *Set your pace.*

Let's not spiritually glide along, drifting aimlessly. We have purpose. We have power. We are women on a mission to obtain the prize—and it is not celery. Run, girlfriend, run!

What is weighing you down and tripping you up on your race?

See if any of these are on your list:

Comparisons. Comparisons hinder our calling, every single time. Our goal is the finish line, God's eternal rewards. Let's keep our eyes focused straight ahead, not evaluating ourselves against others. *Your race, your pace.* You just keep giving it your all.

Complaining. *It's hard. I can't do it. I'm old.* Those things may be true, but it's time to fill your mind with truth!

> *I can do all things through Christ!*
>
> *I am never alone!*
>
> *I have all the power I need for all the challenges I face!*

If you find yourself struggling, please call a godly girlfriend and say, "I'm running this race, but I'm weary. Can you cheer me on and remind me God's got this and I'm not alone?"

Coasting. We don't have time for drifting aimlessly. We live in a lost, broken, and hurting world desperate for the light and love of Jesus. We need every brother and sister to run his/her race with passion and purpose.

🌼 *Have a training program in place.*

 How spiritually fit are you? What training exercises do you have in place? We won't be runners if we don't train. Which of the following do you need to add into your program? Circle them.

Daily quiet time	Scripture memory
Small group and accountability	Fasting
Prayer	Serving your local church
Mentoring a new believer	Solitude

What spiritual disciplines have helped you grow the most on your faith journey? What is one thing you can implement this week in your spiritual training program?

Define your race. Set your pace. Have a training program in place. And if you stumble, get back in the race. The good news is—there is always grace!

PART FIVE:
Finishing Well

Memory Verse: Be careful, however, that the exercise of your rights does not become a stumbling block to the weak.

—1 Corinthians 8:9

The headlines are the worst:

> "Mega-Church Pastor Caught Raiding His Church's Cookie Jar"

> "Christian DJ Sentenced to Life in Prison for Criminal Sexual Misconduct"

> "Family Values-Touting Reality Star Busted for Porn Addiction"

Recent years have been painful for the worldwide Christian community as high-profile Christian leaders have fallen into sin time and again. Brothers and sisters with powerful potential to spread the gospel get sucked down the tubes of temptation, and their testimony is broken in pieces. The world mocks them gleefully, pouncing on the fact that these famous Christians' message did not match their personal choices. And we, as their sisters and brothers of the faith, grieve and get angry and frustrated—maybe even defensive. It's hard to see the name of Jesus Christ dragged through the mud of people's broken lives. We want to shout from the rooftops—"We're not all like that! Many of us actually care about representing our faith well!"

Although God forgives the tarnished Christian and removes the taint for eternity, the world has a long memory. We wish people would forget, but sinful actions can discredit someone and ruin their testimony, sometimes for as long as they live. The depravity they allowed themselves to get tugged into—choice by little choice— eventually "disqualified" them from being useful to the kingdom.

Yesterday we learned about the roots of Paul's famous "run the race" analogy.

 Review 1 Corinthians 9:24–27. Write verse 27 below, underlining the word *disqualified*.

The Greek word in 1 Corinthians 9:27 that is commonly translated as *disqualified* is *adokimos*, and it was often used to refer to contaminated coins and metals. Specifically, it was used to describe materials that, when tested for integrity, were found to be impure. When used to describe a person, *adokimos* means he/she has been tested and is no longer an approved person, or is unfit for service.[9]

Disqualified. Disapproved. Discredited. Unfit.

 What image do you think of when you hear the word *disqualified*?

Digging Deeper

What did Paul mean when he said, "I myself will not be disqualified . . ."? What was he advising the Corinthians, and you and me in our misguided world today? Is there a way to "disqualify-proof" our lives? What's the secret to finishing our race well?

First, let's clear up what he *wasn't* talking about. Paul's fear was *not* that he might lose his salvation, his place in the family of God. He knew that brothers and sisters of the faith are eternally secure in the Lord Jesus Christ.[10] Yet Paul was aware he could fall away from his closeness with Christ and lose his effectiveness in life and ministry. He was also concerned he would suffer the loss of rewards (remember eternal rewards, not perishable celery) as well as be "ashamed at Christ's coming" at the judgment seat of Christ.[11]

But if Paul—who had seen Jesus with his own two eyes—had predetermined to stay pure and upright to the end, we'd be wise to follow his example. We must imitate his resolute mind-set and develop a "finishing well" strategy and plan.

Let's be real: starting the race is simple. Many believers begin the Christian life with fresh passion, enthusiasm, and devotion. They buy the bumper stickers, sport the cross tattoo, recite the right lingo, and sing the upbeat songs. They pray and read their Bible regularly, and join their Christian clubs.

But before long, life kicks in. Without a purposeful plan, it's easy to fall into lukewarm habits or behaviors, slowly tire of the effort, and carelessly let down one's guard.

"Quiet time? Not anymore. Mornings are the only time all day I get to myself, so I like to catch up with my coffee and Facebook friends. When life slows down, I'll have a better routine."

"Scripture Memory? No thanks. I'm not good at memorizing. Who does that anymore?"

"Do we have a new church home? Not right now—our Sundays are packed! But we've found a good online church to watch when we can, so we're good. Thanks."

It doesn't matter how you start, friend. The key is to stay strong to the end. I mean, let's consider Demas. In Colossians 4:14, Demas is listed right alongside Luke as sending greetings to the church of Colossae. (Luke, as in the author of Luke and Acts. Wow.) In Philemon 24, Demas is referred to as a coworker of the apostle Paul. Wouldn't that be a cool way to be remembered in the Bible?

Turn to 2 Timothy 4:9–10. How is Demas identified? Where was Demas focusing his attention when Paul sent this correspondence to Timothy?

Oh, Demas. Most scholars believe he ditched Paul, dumped his faith, and foolishly succumbed to the lures of the world. What a heartbreaking legacy. Clearly it doesn't matter how you begin your race—Demas started well. Our past performances do not guarantee future faithfulness.

So, how do we make certain that we, unlike Demas, do not get disqualified from our race? Paul shares an important insight in the same letter written to his beloved disciple Timothy.

 Read 2 Timothy 2:5 and write Paul's wisdom below.

Let me explain more fully. While John and I toured the ancient site of the Isthmian Games, we saw the foundations of the fourth-century temple of Poseidon, the traces of the archaic stadium, plus the stone theater used for the athletic competitions. It was at this archaic site that Professor Gordon Franz opened my eyes with these insights:

> A small structure called the Palaimon was situated near the Poseidon temple. Within this structure, the athlete took an oath to abide by the rules of the Games. If they broke the oath, they were disqualified from the Games . . . .
>
> Most likely Paul had in mind the oaths that the athletes took in the underground cave of the Palaimon [when he penned 2 Timothy 2:5]. Here, the athletes swore that they would follow the rules in their training as well as not cheat in order to win the

Isthmian crown. In the Christian "race," we must follow the rules as well. In order to know what the rules are, one must know the "Rule Book," the Word of God. It behooves the believer in the Lord Jesus to read, study, and apply the Word of God to his/her life.[12]

If the athletes broke the oath, they were what? Circle the word in the last sentence of the first paragraph of the quote.

What wisdom does Professor Franz call believers to apply if we want to run our Christian race well and not be disqualified? Underline his advice in the second paragraph of the quote.

I think Professor Franz is reminding us that to "disqualify-proof" our life we need to *know* and *live* the truth! Would you agree?

Do you know someone who is no longer running the Christian race?

Unfortunately, I do. In fact, this woman was once my mentor and confidante. When I came to know Christ, the woman who introduced me to Jesus also introduced me to "Maggie." Maggie, who had been a drug and alcohol addict as well, was a beautiful, tender-hearted woman just a few years older than me. "I would never guess you were a cocaine addict," I said when I saw her face-to-face for the first time.

"I would have never guessed *you* were a cocaine addict," she replied. That was it: we were kindred spirits.

Maggie and I spent every afternoon together for many months after I accepted Christ. Maggie was my lifeline. She was committed to helping me walk out my new life with Christ—victoriously. She was always there for me.

In fact, if I tried to cancel on our plans, she would hunt me down. Maggie somehow knew that if I was canceling on her, my thoughts might be headed down a slippery slope. Many times, she was right. I don't know what I would have done without Maggie by my side—coaching me, believing in me like few others did.

Maggie was also the first person who encouraged me to share my story at church. Soon after, as more opportunities emerged, she accompanied me to every one of my speaking engagements. I could count on Maggie—right there in the front row—making sure I was prepared and prayed over before I stood behind the podium, always.

About three years into our journey together, I noticed Maggie didn't want to come to my speaking engagements anymore. She was too busy to get together. Whenever I called her, she would talk on and on about her new thing—yoga. (I am not saying yoga is bad; it's a gray area.) Maggie was captivated with yoga; it seemed to control her life. I worried I was losing my friend and didn't know what to do. We were definitely not on the same page anymore.

I'll never forget the day my fears were confirmed. I was pregnant with my son, and I was feeling kind of frumpy. The old lies were coming back to taunt me. I called my mentor and said, "Can you help me?" Like old times, Maggie rushed right over.

Do you know someone who is no longer running the Christian race?

Only this time, after listening to my concerns, she said, "Don't worry, Cindy, someday you'll have abs like these." She lifted up her shirt and showed me her impressive, made-of-marble abs.

I thought, "Oh Lord, what has happened to this woman?" I mean, she had great abs. But the old Maggie would have pointed me to truth. She would have said I was beloved, chosen, and oh so cherished. She would have made me write out Bible verses and prayed God's promises over me.

Soon after, Maggie opened up her own yoga studio. Later I heard through the grapevine she left her husband. Today, she is remarried and living a very "free-thinking" life in another state. My sense is she has dropped out of the race completely.

Let's all of us—you and me and all our sisters and brothers—make sure that we follow the rules of the race, let go of anything and everything that is tripping us up, and predetermine to stay qualified to finish this race well.

 Apply It

I love 2 Corinthians 13:5 in the New King James Version:

> *Test yourselves to see if you are in the faith; examine yourselves! Or do you not recognize this about yourselves, that Jesus Christ is in you—unless you are disqualified.*

Is there anything in your life right now that could disqualify you from running toward the finish line? Something you're trying to keep hidden from friends and family? Something you're trying to keep concealed from God? (Keep in mind: He already knows.)

Here's what I want you to do:

1. *Tell someone.*

Do you have a trusted friend or Christian counselor with whom you could share your struggles? May I also encourage you to find someone with whom you can develop a consistent accountability relationship? You may want to develop four or five standard weekly questions that this person can ask you, such as:

🌸 Have you given Jesus first place in your life this week?

🌸 Have you spent quality time seeking to *know, live, and share the truth?*

🌸 Have you demonstrated love to your family this week? How?

🌸 What sins are weighing you down or tripping you up?

✿ Have you just lied to me?

We all need Godly accountability in our lives if our desire is to *live full* and *walk free*. We are not meant to journey alone!

2. *Visualize the consequences.*

I often say to my kids, "Don't do anything you wouldn't want on the front page of the newspaper." I hold myself to the same standard.

Think about the choices in your life that, if not dealt with, could disqualify you from finishing well. Imagine the worst-case scenario! For example, if you struggle with viewing impure images, picture someone finding your search history and sharing it on Facebook, or bringing it before your boss. Once you have the worst-case scenario in mind, fill in the newspaper headline below.

3. *Repent.*

Find a scrap piece of paper and pour out your heart to God. Confess the secret sins, the worldliness, lack of self-control, and/or anything else that could develop into an obstacle or hindrance from concluding your race victoriously. Use Psalm 51 as a guide to lead you in a prayer of confession, and then destroy your paper. Remember, you confess it and He forgives it!

The good news: it's never too late to come home and get back in the race. I'm believing by faith "Maggie" will turn back to her First Love. Will you join me in praying that prayer?

 Who do you know who has been disqualified due to immoral or worldly choices? Confidentially write their initials below.

Let's pray God will set them free from anything/everything that is not from Him, clean them up, fill them afresh with His power, and put them back in the race with a faith-filled finish line in sight. Failure does not have to be the final word for any of God's family members!

Remember, it's easy to start but harder to finish. Someday when we stand before our nail-scarred Savior, He's not going to say, "Well start." Instead, may we hear . . .

"Well done, good and faithful servant. Well done!" —Matthew 25:21

Video Lesson Five:
TO EAT OR NOT TO EAT

Use the space below to note anything that stands out to you from the video lesson. You may also choose to take notes on a separate sheet of paper.

Use the following questions as a guide for group discussion:

1. What stood out to you in today's video teaching? Any new insights?

2. Can you think of a situation where you were faced with a gray area? How might Paul's wisdom in 1 Corinthians 8 have helped you decide whether or not to engage in a permissible activity?

3. How would you describe a "stumbling block"? What do the following verses teach us about stumbling blocks: Romans 14:1–3, 12–13? Can you think of an example in your own life where you have been impacted by a stumbling block?

4. Cindy's challenge was to put an ace of hearts playing card somewhere to remind you that "love trumps knowledge." Is there a specific situation or relationship where you're most tempted to forget that you can be right and still be wrong?

5. How might the four questions Cindy shared help you make the best decision the next time you are faced with a gray area?

CHAPTER SIX

Our Final Victory

Prayer:

O God, You are faithful, strong, and good. Help me to keep my eyes focused on Jesus, and not on anyone and everyone else. Lord, when the things of this world start weighing me down and tripping me up, remind me of the rewards waiting for me at the finish line. How I long for the day I hear Jesus say, "Well done, good and faithful servant." As I begin this last week of study, please teach me new things from Your Word. Reveal fresh insights about who You are and who I am to You. Empower me to put into practice what I am learning. I don't want to just *hear* the Word, God; I want to *live* Your Word. Thank You for your goodness and grace. I am delighted to be Your daughter. In Jesus' name. Amen.

PART ONE:
The Struggle Bus

Memory Verse: Be on your guard; stand firm in the faith; be courageous; be strong. Do everything in love.

—1 Corinthians 16:13–14

Have you ever let your frazzled feelings lead you to make choices you later regretted?

Yeah, me too.

I was recently talking with my friend Jamie after she'd had a *looong*, disappointing Monday. Everywhere she turned she was pelted with lies, frustration, and discouragement. To switch gears, she decided to focus on someone other than herself and bake cookies for a sick friend. Jamie's watching her weight, so her plan was to eat half a fresh-baked cookie as a treat.

The trouble began with the smell—buttery and sugary—you know the heavenly aroma. Jamie walked away for a few minutes and was quickly distracted. When she returned to the kitchen, the smell had changed from butter and sugar to char and scorch. Half of the cookies were burned, and the other half too burned to give away. Slumping over in tears of frustration, Jamie caved in and inhaled half a batch of half burned cookies.

Easy comfort, right? Except every woman knows what really happened: After eating those cookies, Jamie carried guilt and shame on top of everything else that had gone wrong in her life on that horrible, rotten, no-good day.

I have so been there. My guess is, you have too.

One more cookie story, because in this life we will have cookie temptations.

Once, when my kids were ages one, two, three, and ten, I came up with the brilliant idea to invite all the fourth-grade moms from my son's school over for coffee, conversation, and homemade chocolate chip cookies.

It seemed like a good idea at the time, but my plan to win friends and influence people through chocolate quickly went bust. In the midst of trying to keep my kiddos busy, roll store-bought dough onto cookie sheets, and frantically hide all our clutter, I gave in and ate (more like "sucked down") four ooey-gooey-warm-and-chewy cookies.

Later that week, when I sunk down into my therapist's couch, I cried and told her that I was disgusted with myself. I was filled with self-loathing and shame. Why? Because of the cookies. I told her that I had been striving to pretend I had it all together, when the reality was I was hanging on by a thread (a thin thread, at that).

And then, longing for connection and acceptance from these other moms, I had tried to numb my feelings with homemade cookies. And afterward, what did I do? I let the enemy flood me with lies and guilt and shame.

My therapist listened and nodded. "Cindy, do you think you are the only woman who has eaten some of her homemade cookies?"

"But I ate *four* cookies. Not one, not two, but *four*." I said it loudly, as if she spoke a foreign language and couldn't understand the meaning of the number four.

"Cindy, do you think you are the only woman who has eaten *four* of her homemade cookies?" my therapist replied.

"Um, yeah, probably not."

So recently, when I listened to my friend Jamie describe her discouragement and self-loathing over eating *her* chocolate chip cookies, I recycled my therapist's question.

"Jamie, do you think you are the only woman who has eaten some of her homemade cookies? Because, friend, you are *not* the only one."

The words I gave Jamie are the words I want to give to you: *You are not the only one.*

You are not the only one who deviated from your healthy eating plan.

You are not the only one who feels disappointed, discouraged, or overwhelmed.

You are not the only one who wonders if you're "not enough" compared to air-brushed perfection.

The struggle is real, friends. In fact, these days people like to say they are "riding the Struggle Bus" when things are just not going their way. When we ride the Struggle Bus, we

Fight.   *Battle.*

Wrestle.   *Resist.*

All of these words describe the effort we sometimes exert to push back at temptation. And I'm not just talking about cookies. Temptation comes in various forms. We might be tempted to . . .

❀ shop 'til we drop, on a secret credit account our husband knows nothing about.

❀ drink a little too much alcohol, to numb our pain.

❀ be seduced by the sweet talk of that cute guy at work who pays more attention to us than our husband does.

Every single day, we fight, wrestle, battle, resist, and struggle.

Paul's beloved Corinthian flock was struggling with temptation too. Some of them, forgetting *they* were the temple, stuffed themselves with rich foods. Several had liquored up despite their determination not to become inebriated again. Certain folks jumped back into bed with a temple prostitute, following the treacherous path stamped "follow me" all the way to sexual immorality.

So how were they to—how are we to—*live full* and *walk free* in a seductive culture where moral decadence and sin-inducing stresses and messes abound? We've talked about our strategy if our temptation is sexual immorality—*flee!* But what if we are tempted by cravings in other areas? Then what?

Thankfully, God's Word does not leave us guessing. Paul's letter to the Corinthians speaks realistically to you, me, and cookie lovers everywhere about how to live strong amid all the temptations surrounding us.

Digging Deeper

Read 1 Corinthians 10:1–13 and summarize Paul's words from verses 12 and 13 below.

Paul, being Paul, a practical kind of guy, recognized it wasn't easy to live sin-free in Sin City—*but it was possible!* In an effort to persuade his beloved brothers and sisters to avoid the sparkly temptations and traps of the world, he started off with a history lesson: the story of the Israelites in the desert.

All God's children, said Paul, shared in the goodness of God's provision and protection in the wilderness. (You may want to circle every occurrence of the word *all* in 1 Corinthians 10:1–4 in your Bible. Look what they experienced—wow!) Yet most of them did not finish well. In fact, did you catch verse 5? The Message paraphrases it this way:

> *But just experiencing God's wonder and grace didn't seem to mean much— most of them were defeated by temptation during the hard times in the desert, and God was not pleased.*

Imagine ending up rotting as washed-out bones in the desert, all because you gave in to temptation. Yikes.

So Paul delivered a stern warning to his brothers and sisters and then reminded them—and us—that this doesn't have to be how our story ends! There is another way. (And everyone said, "Phew!")

"No temptation has overtaken you except what is common to mankind" (v. 13a).

In other words, you are not the only one.

Paul wanted the individuals on the Struggle Bus to understand this, because sin grows in seclusion. If we think we are the only one with a particular disordered desire, we'll be less likely to share our struggles or ask for help. Secrets keep us stuck.

Sin grows in seclusion.

So the first key to overcoming temptation is remembering that you are not the only one. And the second is remembering our trustworthy, dependable, believable God.

"And God is faithful; he will not let you be tempted beyond what you can bear" (v. 13b).

God will never allow His followers to encounter an unconquerable temptation. Never! Instead He does this:

"But when you are tempted, he will also provide a way out so that you can endure it" (v. 13c).

Notice Paul said *when* we are tempted, not *if.* Temptations are a part of living in our broken, sin-soaked world. It's not a sin to be tempted; even Jesus was tempted.[1] Being tempted basically means we're normal. Temptation is not cause for feeling guilty, embarrassed, defeated, or condemned. Temptation is a sacred moment for standing firm in our faith and making a God-honoring choice.

No matter how flashy Satan's lure is, Paul tells us that temptation is 100 percent conquerable! Temptations can be withstood. There is no temptation without a plan of escape! It was true for the Corinthians and it's true for us. Help is not only on its way; it's already here with us, now.

Here's a personal story from video lesson four that bears repeating.

You know about my multi-year battle with drug and alcohol addiction. Even after I was saved and living a sober life, there was still a "hook" with my name on it: cocaine. It was like I was the fish, and cocaine was the shiniest, most enticing lure in the whole wide ocean of choices.

About four months into my sobriety, little lies began to pop in my head regarding my old drug of choice. Suddenly it seemed so appealing to use again. Surely, the doctors had been overly dramatic about my overdose. It wasn't that bad—right?

The road to sin begins in our thought life, friends. It really does.

I called my old dealer one night and begged him to sell me some cocaine. He absolutely refused. He said that I was a "Jesus Freak" now, and that freaked him out!

That was Way Out #1.

But I wanted those drugs—badly. I decided to drive to a location where I knew I could make a purchase.

Way Out #2 came as I walked out my door and found my friend standing there with movies in one hand and snacks in the other. God had impressed upon her good listening heart that she needed to keep me inside my house that night, for my own protection.

The enticement of cocaine was a shiny lure Satan had cast my way. My own willpower was obviously not enough to resist that strong of a hook. (Willpower alone never works, trust me.) However, the temptation did not overpower me. God made a way!

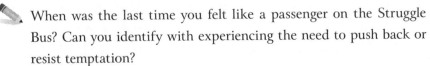

Apply It

When was the last time you felt like a passenger on the Struggle Bus? Can you identify with experiencing the need to push back or resist temptation?

Are there specific temptations that threaten to "overtake" you most often? Circle any/all from the following list:

Overspending	Drug use
Jealousy	Worldliness
Greed	Stealing
Alcohol abuse	Discontentment
Pornography	Testing God
Materialism	Lies
Gossip	Sexual immorality
Numbing out	Binging/purging
Anger/rage	Self-absorption
Perfectionism	Laziness
Overeating	Overuse of TV and/or social media
Critical spirit	Other:
Comparisons	

How are you presently seeking to overcome this area of temptation? How might *knowing* and *living* 1 Corinthians 10:13 help you on your journey as you *live full* and *walk free*?

Fill in your name in 1 Corinthians 10:13 below. Read it aloud as a declaration of truth, as well as a prayer. You may want to write it on an index card and keep it on hand in your areas of greatest temptation.

"No temptation has overtaken _____
except what is common to mankind. And God is faithful; he will not let
_____ *be tempted beyond what*
_____ *can bear. But when*
_____ *is tempted, He will also*
provide a way out so that _____ *can*
endure it."

Aren't you thankful for a loving Father, a risen Savior, and the empowering Holy Spirit to help you endure *any* and *all* temptations on life's journey? Take a moment and thank God for being your ever present help in time of need (Psalm 46:1).

PART TWO:
Walk Free

Memory Verse: Be on your guard; stand firm in the faith; be courageous; be strong. Do everything in love.

—1 Corinthians 16:13–14

I recently celebrated an amazing milestone: July 26, 2016 marked my twentieth anniversary of being cocaine-free. *Twenty years!* Praise God!

I could never have experienced victory over my addiction without God's faithfulness. He truly has provided "a way out" so I could endure being tempted, time and time again.

Whether our temptation is cocaine or cookies, social media or shopping, ex-boyfriends or ex-habits, our inheritance is not to live in a polluted pit of self-defeat, condemnation, and despair. Jesus came so we can "enjoy life, and have it in abundance [to the full, till it overflows]" (John 10:10 AMP). Not just when we get to heaven someday, but *today!*

Jesus alone can rescue and redeem, deliver and restore, open up the prison gates and set any captive free—including me, including *you!*

But what is our role—if any—when the enemy's flashy lure is cast our way? When God says He will "make a way," does that mean we have *no* responsibility? Can we just lounge on the sofa waiting for God to airlift us out whenever we feel tempted to compare, overspend, or scarf down that hot fudge sundae? What's our part to play—if any—to experience victory in the midst of our daily temptations and trials?

✣ Digging Deeper

Let's start with reviewing Paul's practical encouragement for the Corinthians, who were surrounded with constant temptations of immorality, idolatry, and indulgence.

 Review 1 Corinthians 10:13 below, as quoted from the Amplified Bible. Circle occurrences of the word *temptation* and underline anything else that stands out to you.

> *No temptation [regardless of its source] has overtaken or enticed you that is not common to human experience [nor is any temptation unusual or beyond human resistance]; but God is faithful [to His word—He is compassionate and trustworthy], and He will not let you be tempted beyond your ability [to resist], but along with the temptation He [has in the past and is now and] will [always] provide the way out as well, so that you will be able to endure it [without yielding, and will overcome temptation with joy].*

[God] will not let you be tempted beyond your ability [to resist].

—1 Corinthians 10:13 AMP

What a power-packed verse! I think it belongs on my refrigerator. Not only is a high-calorie treat not the boss of me, I can pass on the potato chips with joy! Who knew?!

The word *temptation* is the Greek word *peirasmos*, which refers not only to temptations but to trials and testings as well. (In fact, some Bibles translate *peirasmos* as a test or trial, and others as a temptation.[2])

Look up the following verses and match each one with what we can learn about temptation:

Luke 4:13 •   • Don't be surprised if you are tempted.

Matthew 6:13 •   • We should pray to not be led into temptation.

James 1:2 •   • Choose joy when the temptation comes.

James 1:12 •   • The enemy will flee if his plan doesn't work.

1 Peter 4:12 •   • There's a crown waiting for those who endure temptations.

 What surprises you most from these verses? What else have you learned about temptation?

God doesn't tempt us (James 1:13). But with every temptation God *allows*, there's always the potential we might fall back into sin. We don't have to, though; we always have a choice! "As Christ followers, we fight not *for* our victory but *from* a place of victory."[3] How awesome is that!

 Peek back at the Bible quotation and circle the words *the way out*.

The Greek words translated *the way out* or *escape* is the word *ekbasis*. "This word is a compound of the word '*ek*,' meaning out, and the word '*basin*,' meaning to walk. When they are compounded together, it means to walk out, as to walk out of a difficult place; to walk out of a trap; or to walk out of a place that isn't good for you."[4]

Friends, let's not miss this—right here is our invitation to *walk free!*

If you ask God for help in your moment of temptation, He will show you how to walk out of your difficult place toward fullness and freedom! God helps you resist the test, infuses you with His power, then gives you an escape route so you can get outta Dodge—and fast. That's *His* part.

But you and I, we must do our part too! Our human strength of resolve is no match for Satan's wicked schemes. Instead of arming ourselves with more willpower, we must arm ourselves spiritually. We have a responsibility to pray, make a battle plan, and stand up—steadfast and grounded—when our cravings come trying to knock us down.

As I battled my way toward cocaine addiction recovery, Jesus did deliver me from my pit of self-defeat and despair. But I also had to take responsibility and do my part, including:

1. Pursuing a daily relationship with Jesus Christ through His Word and prayer (John 14:6).

2. Repeatedly renewing my mind with truth (John 8:32; Romans 12:2).

   Remembers, wrong beliefs will lead to wrong actions. We must *know* truth in order to stand up against the devil's sneaky schemes. Even Jesus conquered Satan's temptation in the desert by quoting Scripture aloud (Matthew 4:4–10).

3. Leaving behind the "old" life (Ephesians 4:22–24).

   When we follow Jesus, we become *brand spanking new!* But we must choose to walk out our new life in Christ. For me, this involved quitting my job, letting go of any substance abuse-related friendships, and avoiding any environments where temptations would be high.

4. Exposing my secrets and lies to His light (Ephesians 5:11–14).

5. Getting to the "root" of the problem through godly counseling (Proverbs 15:22; Psalm 147:3).

6. Asking for ongoing accountability and pursuing Christian community (James 5:16).

7. Discovering and practicing new healthy, God-honoring habits (1 Corinthians 10:31; Romans 12:1).

   For me, this included reading the Bible daily, attending church and a weekly Bible study, making new friends, and finding wholesome ways to have fun.

8. Praying.

   I *still* ask God daily to protect me from temptations, replace my cravings with His satisfaction, surround me with women who build me up, and fill my heart and mind with truth (Luke 22:40).

Executing this eight-part strategy was the key to my daily victory. As I asked Jesus to enter into my struggle, it became a collaborative effort, a joint endeavor. In Christ's strength and power, I began making small good decisions, and then choice by choice, I slowly backed away from the cliff and onto solid ground. Willpower alone is not enough, but Jesus is.

Apply It

Let's review the principles to overcoming temptation we've learned. The next time *when* temptation comes your way, I hope you'll be armed and dangerous.

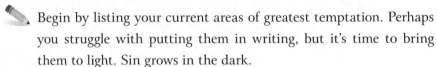 Begin by listing your current areas of greatest temptation. Perhaps you struggle with putting them in writing, but it's time to bring them to light. Sin grows in the dark.

Now reread my eight-step TVP: Temptation Victory Plan. Circle any of the approaches you currently have in place. Write below any of the eight strategies you plan to put into practice.

In addition, here are some questions to consider as you put together your personal TVP.

What triggers set off your urge to sin? What fuels your unhealthy habits?

Satan is a predator, stalking us like a wolf hunts his prey. He looks for the most opportune times to strike, when we are at our weakest. The acronym "HALT" is great for helping us remember to be on our guard during those times we may be at our most vulnerable:

Hungry
Angry
Lonely
Tired

Willpower alone is not enough, but Jesus is.

Write down the situations, times of day, environments, or emotions that most often lead to areas of struggle and temptation for you. How might paying attention to your "trigger time" assist you in your battle against temptation?

If you wait until you are in a high-risk situation to develop your plan to escape temptation, you will struggle. Be proactive. Before the situation occurs, come up with a plan of how to remove yourself from the situation and get support.

 Which godly girlfriend can you share your "TVP" with this week? Write her name below, and come back and put a check by her name when you've shared your victory plan with her.

Don't forget: You are not the only one! It's not a temptation to *want* to sin. It's only a sin if we give in. Your God is faithful. Look for that escape route so you can quickly walk out of that situation and experience victory and freedom. It's time for you to *live full* and *walk free*!

PART THREE:
American Idol

> **Memory Verse:** Be on your guard; stand firm in the faith; be courageous; be strong. Do everything in love.
>
> —1 Corinthians 16:13–14

Recently, a pastor of a church numbering in the tens of thousands was asked to step down by his elder board. The elders cited alcohol abuse and marriage struggles as the reasons for their request.

The pastor apologized publicly in a genuine and remorseful confession. He said, among other things: ". . . in my obsession to do everything possible to reach 100,000 (church attendees) and beyond, it has come at a personal cost in my own life and created a strain on my marriage."[5]

Almost immediately, people started to offer armchair advice through social media. Some helpful; mostly not so helpful. (Lots of puffy stick-whackers.) Yet, one insightful man graciously shared, "While people are wringing their hands over his confessed abuse of alcohol (a problem, to be sure), it appears to be a symptom, not a cause. Meanwhile, I'm afraid we're going to miss . . . the reason for his failure, because we don't want to see it. . . . His obsession to reach '100,000 and beyond' does not excuse his self-confessed sins. By his own admission, it caused them."[6]

While everyone else was laser focused on the symptoms—alcohol misuse and a strained marriage, this man identified the deeper issue: this pastor to thousands had an "obsession" with numbers, and this was the root cause of his being sidelined in his race. Building a church of 100,000 became this pastor's idol.

Idol: an object of worship; a false god; object of extreme devotion (i.e., movie star idol); pretender, impostor.[7]

I didn't immediately spot this pastor's idol because his idols look different than mine. Years ago, drugs and alcohol were my idols—my objects of worship that motivated and drove my behavior. I didn't know that God was enough to fill the canyons in my soul. And sometimes, I still forget that. When I'm sad, anxious, or lonely, I am much more vulnerable to making a *lesser thing*—like lattes, approval, and social media—*the main thing*.

 Can you relate? Have you ever struggled with false objects of devotion in your life?

Let's travel back to idolatrous Corinth for a lesson on lesser gods. Paul had plenty to say throughout his Corinthian correspondence regarding the worship of pagan pretenders and impostors. In Corinth, idols were everywhere and temples abounded. Today, most of us don't put our trust in statues of stone, clay, or wood; but our American idols—power, pleasure, Pinterest, and prestige (to name a few)—are worshiped and adored all the same. Paul knew *all* idols must be dethroned for Christ followers to *live full* and *walk free*.

Digging Deeper

We've learned that in ancient Corinth there was definitely no shortage of gods to bow down to. Pick a pagan god, any pagan god, and chances are you could worship it—whether Aphrodite, Apollo, Poseidon, or Asclepius—in Corinth.

For example, you'll recall Asclepius was the Greek god of healing. If you had a medical need, you'd take a trip over to the temple of Asclepius and petition his help. Remember what you'd bring along?

Yes, a clay replica of the body part in question! If you sprained your foot, you would grab a mud mock-up and head to the temple. Such an ordinary part of life, you wouldn't even think twice about it—like heading to the dentist for a toothache.

When John and I went to the Corinthian museum, we saw a number of the clay replicas that have been excavated in Corinth. Arms, feet, hands, even "private parts." In fact, scholars wonder if these replicas were on Paul's mind when he called the church the "body" of Christ.

Because idolatry was so ingrained in Corinth's culture, believers were having a hard time leaving behind idol worship at the temples. Their old idolatrous habits were hard to shake. Perhaps they had thoughts like:

> *Apollo isn't real, so it won't hurt if I go along with my sister-in-law to keep her company.*

> *God knows my heart. How else will I reach my wine-worshiping buddies and tell them about Jesus, if I skip all the idol feasts?*

> *Look, my baby is sick. What's wrong with trying to get all the help I can? I'll try anything! What do I have to lose?*

Pastor Paul knew the church needed a wake-up call—and fast. They had given their lives to Jehovah Rapha, the God Who Heals. It was time they placed their whole hearts and entire bodies in *His* safekeeping, not in the "healing powers" of a counterfeit idol.

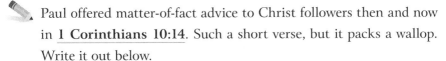

Paul offered matter-of-fact advice to Christ followers then and now in **1 Corinthians 10:14**. Such a short verse, but it packs a wallop. Write it out below.

Let's look at this weighty sentence a portion at a time:

First of all, *"Therefore . . ."* Whenever you come to a *therefore* in the Bible, check to see what it's *there for*. Take it as a clue that whatever is about to be communicated is based on what's already been said. In this case, Paul was wrapping up his warning about how the church's Israelite ancestors had compromised and been damaged by idols.

 Review 1 Corinthians 10:1–13, and then summarize verse 7 below.

 The idolatry Paul was referring to took place in Exodus 32. Hold your place in 1 Corinthians, and **flip to Exodus 32:1–10**. Record some of the sinful, idolatrous choices the Israelites made.

Talk about an outdoor adventure gone wrong: a wild party, lust, drunkenness, and gross immorality; not to mention the idol—a golden calf—the Israelites made and worshiped in the wilderness. Wow.

Next, Paul used the affectionate term *"dear friends"* in (10:14), inferring a loving tone—like a concerned big brother. He had grace for the Corinthians; he had lived among them and knew firsthand how hard it was to break free from their culture.

"Flee from idolatry." Paul's favorite exit strategy: *flee!* Run as fast as you can, as if your badly behaved dog put a dead mouse on your pillow. *Flee from false gods—pronto!* Paul knew you cannot worship an impostor if you're running away from it. Go!

Paul desperately wanted the Corinthians to be gravely serious about the risks of idolatry. Putting anything ahead of God has the potential to destroy lives, marriages, and ministries. Friend, this has not changed in two thousand years.

 Look up the following verses and give main points on what the Bible says about idolatry:

Exodus 20:3–6

Isaiah 44:9–20

Matthew 6:24

Colossians 3:5

"Most of us think of an idol as a statue of wood, stone, or metal worshiped by pagan people," writes Ken Sande. "In biblical terms, it is something other than God that we set our heart on, that motivates us, that masters and rules us, or that we trust, fear, or serve."[8]

Therefore, if you and I are really serious about *living full* and *walking free*, we too must dethrone the idols in our lives. I'm not talking about pocket-sized obsessions, like a game on your phone or a favorite salty snack. I'm talking about those things and people on which we set our hope.

What and who is getting first place in your life?

 ## Apply It

 Remember what the megachurch pastor said? "In my obsession to do everything possible to reach 100,000 and beyond . . ." His idol was building a huge church. What is yours?

How would you fill in the pastor's sentence for yourself?

"In my obsession to do everything possible to _____

_____."

Would you fill that blank with . . .

. . . receive the approval of a certain friend, family member, boss, or group of people you are desperate to please?

. . . gain a particular possession or new level of financial security?

. . . reach a career objective or a personal goal?

Idolatry is being obsessed with or putting your hope in a created thing rather than the God who created all. Bible teacher Kelly Minter shares, "Too often we profess God but look to everything else to function as him. Even perfectly good things. Things that in and of themselves are pure and right and gifts from God but have become a problem simply because of the placement they have in our lives."[9]

 Spend time reflecting on idols. Is there anything getting first place in your life that needs to be dethroned? How might God want you to respond based on what you've learned from His life-changing Word today? Journal your thoughts:

God, I love You. I acknowledge that I wrestle with keeping First things First. Forgive me, Father. You are so worthy of all of my praise! I confess I have put _____ before You. I choose to smash down, dethrone, and remove this idol, which competes with my affection for You. Fill my mind with a fresh revelation of who You are, Lord. Teach me how to order my life so You are first and foremost, always. May I be a one-God woman. In the loving name of Jesus, my powerful Savior I pray. Amen.

PART FOUR:
Love Is . . .

> **Memory Verse:** Be on your guard; stand firm in the faith; be courageous; be strong. Do everything in love.
>
> —1 Corinthians 16:13–14

I pasted a smile on my face as a couple thousand people in my church sanctuary cheered for me, hooting and hollering. They were standing to their feet. It was my last Sunday as children's ministry director at my church, and the pastor had just finished praying for me. Anyone would have thought the applause and a standing ovation would have blessed my socks off—but actually it had the opposite effect.

When I got off the stage and wandered down a hallway, a man stopped me in my tracks. "You must feel so loved right now," he said brightly as he shook my hand enthusiastically. However, truth be told, I felt broken inside. I was leaving my leadership role at the church for which I cared deeply, and would be focusing all my attention at home. I thought God was going to use my story to change lives around the world, but instead I was "promoted" to changing diapers, onesies, and bed sheets. God had called me to this season of transition, but it didn't mean there wasn't an inner struggle.

"You must feel so loved right now." How often I've thought about the irony in the man's words.

Loved.

What does it mean to feel loved? What does it mean to love somebody?

I don't know about you, but I throw that word around mighty easily.

I *love* Mexican food. I *love* coffee. I *love* being a hockey mom. On and on I use the word *love*, tossing it around like an almost weightless Frisbee—wispy, floaty, fluffy.

This is what we do, don't we? It's easy to love everything!

 Jot down items on your love list:

I mean, there are love bugs, love seats, and love boats. And love notes, love songs, and love birds.

You can be lovesick, loveless, and lovely.

You can fall in it, be addicted to it, play the game of love, with the power of love

There's even a "love chapter" in the Bible, and it happens to be near the end of Paul's letter to those sometimes loveless Corinthians. We've heard it read and expounded on many times, mostly at weddings. My husband John even had it written on an index card when he proposed to me! It's one of the most memorized, well-liked, and well-known passages in all of Scripture, even by non-church folk. In fact, we've heard this famous passage so often it's tempting for our eyes to glaze over. "Love is patient, love is kind . . ." Yeah, yeah. We know.

> *Lovelessness was a root spiritual problem in the Corinthian church.*

Yet wedding sermons, cross-stitched pillows, and even proposal inspiration was not Paul's intent when he wrote those famous words. Paul was actually not "feeling the love," if you know what I mean.

Instead, Paul was reprimanding a seriously messed-up church for their massive lack of love. That's right, the "love chapter" is really a rebuke—a scold, a critique, and a serious talking to! Lovelessness was a root spiritual problem in the Corinthian church.

How in the world have we gotten this passage flipped upside down for two thousand years? It's time to get flipped right side up again. We can't ignore the real context of this chapter. If we do, we are in danger of missing its crucial message.

Digging Deeper

 Take a few moments to **read 1 Corinthians 13:1–13**. Ask God to open your eyes to see this passage with a fresh perspective, and to encounter new, wonderful things in His Word (Psalm 119:18). Record the characteristics of love Paul recorded in verses 4–8.

Do those words sound like the characteristics of the Christ followers in Corinth? Um, not so much. Unfortunately, the church members in Corinth had bombed in love, over and over. In fact, many of their failure-to-love behaviors were the first requirements of love Paul mentioned in the love chapter.

Paul was saying, "Friends, you have failed—sometimes spectacularly—at acting out the true meaning of love. You've shown yourselves to be jealous, bragging, puffed up, and self-absorbed to a ridiculous degree. You've been total love flops. Let's talk about how you can flourish in love."

So Paul took them deep into the gritty heart of love and the way of Jesus (which, of course, has very little to do with weddings, Christian décor, or wispy, floaty, and fluffy feelings).

It's time for a love lesson. Let's take a look at the nuances of the word for *love* used in 1 Corinthians 13.

The Greeks had at least three different words for love, each describing a different aspect of it. Since we have only one word for love in English, it gets confusing unless we learn the uniqueness of each

Greek word. We love Jesus and guacamole and shopping at Target. See the complication?

When writing the love chapter, Paul did *not* use the Greek word *eros*, which is swoony and dazzling and hormone-based. (It's where we get the English word *erotic*.) *Eros* describes how we feel when we are falling madly in love—the sexual, romantic attraction. In reality, that word never appears in the entire Bible.

Do you love anyone with *eros* love? (If so, I hope you're married. Or you may want to go back to Chapter 4. Just kidding, kind of.)

Neither did Paul use the word *philia*, which refers to fondness, warmth, and brotherly love. The closest word in English would probably be *friendship*. In fact, the city Philadelphia was named by William Penn using two Greek words: *philia*, "friendship," and *adelphos*, "brother."[10] Penn had faced religious persecution and wanted his colony to be a place where anyone could worship freely. To remember *philia*, think Philadelphia—the City of Brotherly Love!

 David and Jonathan are an excellent illustration of *philia* love in the Bible.[11] Who are the women/men in your life you love with a friendship love?

The word for love Paul *does* use in 1 Corinthians 13 is intentional and careful, a solid and hefty word to teach us how to love through the ages: *agape*. This is the word used most often in the New Testament to demonstrate the perfect love of God. Greek scholar Rick Renner writes:

> Paul uses the word *agape* to describe the highest level of love in this world . . . a love so completely different from what the world offers that it is only used in the New Testament to describe God's love and the love that should flow from the hearts of believers. *Agape*

is a divine love that gives and gives and gives, even if it's never responded to, thanked, or acknowledged. You could say that *agape* is a love that isn't based on response but on a decision to keep on loving, regardless of a recipient's response or lack of response. Because *agape* is such an unconditional love, I call it high-level love. It is the highest, most noble, purest form of love that exists.[12]

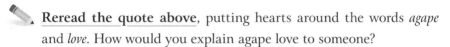 **Reread the quote above**, putting hearts around the words *agape* and *love*. How would you explain agape love to someone?

Find the following verses in your Bible and write down what additional nuggets of goodness you learn about God's agape love:

John 3:16

John 15:9

Romans 5:5

Romans 8:38–39

1 John 3:1

Do you understand how loved you are?

Do you get it? God. Loves. You! Yes, *you!*

God loves you so much that He sent Jesus to Earth—for you! In fact, you could reread the love chapter with Jesus' name in place of *love* starting in 1 Corinthians 13:4. Jesus is patient. Jesus is kind . . . Jesus never fails.

Regardless of what you have done—or what has been done to you; in spite of your sins and shortcomings; whatever your past problems or poor choices might have been—He loves you! And what can separate you from God's love?

 Peek back at Romans 8:39 if you have already forgotten, and then write it in all caps below.

He loves you—not *when* you lose the weight or get out of debt, or *will* love you if you start having more quiet time or memorize your verses, or *used* to love you before the divorce. He agape, "high-power level," no-strings-attached, loves you!

🌿 Apply It

One of my grandma's much loved songs was the '70s classic, "Feelings."[13] There's wisdom in this tune, at least in the "nothing more than feelings" lyric. So often our feelings of love are nothing more than a mood or a fickle frame of mind. As I study 1 Corinthians 13, I am struck by the complete absence of emphasis on personal feelings. How we feel is truly beside the point here. The truth is: whether we "feel" loved or not, we are loved. Period.

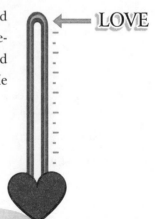

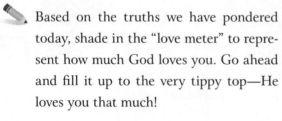 Based on the truths we have pondered today, shade in the "love meter" to represent how much God loves you. Go ahead and fill it up to the very tippy top—He loves you that much!

Author Max Lucado writes, "If God had a refrigerator, your picture would be on it. If He had a wallet, your photo would be in it. He sends you flowers every spring and a sunrise every morning. . . . Face it, friend. He is crazy about you!"[14]

If you are in a place where you don't *feel* loved, grab some notecards and write today's agape love verses out to remind you of the capital "T" Truth—you are loved. There isn't anything you can do to make Him love you more, and there isn't anything you can do to make Him love you less. Now that's amazing love!

 Review the list of love characteristics from 1 Corinthians 13. Think of at least one special person who has demonstrated God's agape love to you. Spend a few moments thanking God for their example and love, using the space below. Consider sending them a love note or text to remind them of how much they mean to you.

PART FIVE:
Final Greetings

Memory Verse: Be on your guard; stand firm in the faith; be courageous; be strong. Do everything in love.

—1 Corinthians 16:13–14

I remember dropping my firstborn Jake off at kindergarten like it was yesterday. His new cartoon-themed backpack was packed with fresh school supplies, and his nutritious, delicious lunch was lovingly prepared and bundled in his Space Jam lunchbox. Oh, the anxiety, the tears, the ripping sensation one experiences in one's chest! Okay, so that was just me, not my boy. Jake was fine!

But still. First days of school are a big milestone—a transition from your child being under your wing to them being on their own. Or, at least he or she is on their own some of the time, because one teacher can't corral those little kiddos every second of every school day. Some independence is required, which begs the question, "Did I as a mom do enough to prepare my beloved son to stand on his own?"

- ❧ Does he know how to find the bathroom, or will he be confident enough to ask if he doesn't?

- ❧ Will he share with his new friends, and be a buddy to anyone feeling left out?

- ❧ Will he say "please" and "thank you" to the teacher, and say a prayer before lunch?

With all four of my kids, I fought back the urge to dispense last-minute advice about hand washing and classroom etiquette. I waved them off, trying to radiate a cheer I did not totally feel. "Bye for now! Have a great day! You can do it! Love you!"

My last word to my kids was *love*, always.

Let's see how Paul wrapped up his letter to those unruly, disagreeable, confused Corinthians. Yes, they were all those things, yet they were made loveable by the One who loved them. Because of God's agape, high-level love, Paul was able to express genuine tenderness to those brothers and sisters who had made his life quite troublesome.

Bear in mind, Pastor Paul and his fickle, fighting sheep had been through a great deal together. He started out his dispatch to them wearing "glasses of grace"—offering the church members a kindness and mercy they did not deserve. With grace as his backdrop, Paul quickly made it clear that the Corinthians still needed a good kick in the togas. They were just like their culture—indulgent, idolatrous, and immoral—on a good day. And they had had some very bad days!

In his letter, Paul issued some strong corrective commands. Get down off your high horse and try being humble for a change. For crying out loud, unite and don't fight. Stop abusing your bodies and treat them with the respect a glorious temple deserves. Flee—bolt!—from a single whiff of sexual immorality.

He also addressed some real nitty-gritty questions about how to *live full* and *walk free* as a set apart, holy, and new creation of God. Corinth was a tough town, chock-full of sticky situations, and Paul knew the brothers and sisters needed to grab hold of practical steps for living in—not avoiding—their worldly surroundings. We need the exact same advice for life in the twenty-first century!

Digging Deeper

Like a mom sending her cherub off on the first day of kindergarten, Paul wanted to sneak in a few final directives, just in case the believers in Corinth might forget what he had taught them. He wanted to make sure one last time that his spiritual children would grow in maturity, even without him physically present or communicating through heartfelt correspondence.

Let's read Paul's final charge: **1 Corinthians 16:13–14**. What were the four farewell commands Paul issued in verse 13? Write them below.

1.

2.

3.

4.

Interestingly, Paul used military metaphors, like a commander ordering his troops.

1. *"Be on your guard."* The Greek *grēgoreō* actually means "to watch."[15] Some Bibles have translated it "be alert"—watchful, vigilant, ready to act. The picture is of a watchman on duty who must be on the alert all the time—which is the opposite of being spiritually careless or easily deceived, as the Corinthians had been acting.

 What are some things Christ followers should be on guard and watch out for? Look up the following verses and write your answers below.

Mark 14:38

1 Peter 5:8

2 Peter 2:1; 1 John 4:1

Matthew 24:42–44

2. *"Stand firm in the faith."* As we've discovered, Paul spent at least eighteen months helping the rookie church in Corinth gain their footing in a slippery society. He grasped that if the believers were going to take their stand in their falling-down world, they needed a firm foundation based on the Word of God. To hold tight to their convictions, they needed to *know* and *live* truth.

In what areas of your life do you find it hardest to stand firm? What lure or temptation is most likely to get you off track?

Paul was saying, "Hey, are you guys going to let the evil one intimidate you, tempt you, and cause your relationships to rip and tear? No way! Lean into God's mighty *dunamis* power, stand on the truth of God's Word, and hold your ground! Don't back down when Satan tries to push you around on life's playground. Take your stand!"

> *Don't back down when Satan tries to push you around on life's playground. Take your stand!*

3. *"Be courageous."* Or, literally, be men and women of courage. Be brave in Jesus' name. Act like a grown-up, mature, settled and established. These days we might call it "adulting."

Then and now, Paul wanted believers to put away immaturity and be responsible for their words, actions, and choices.

 Paul shared similar counsel in **1 Corinthians 14:20**. Summarize Paul's message below:

4. *"Be strong."* The word Paul uses here is the only passive verb in the text, meaning "be strengthened."[15] Let's not get Paul's words twisted: he wasn't demanding that the Corinthians try harder and exert themselves in their own power. (They've been there and done that.[16]) We cannot make ourselves "be strengthened"—that's God's job. Our part is to live surrendered to Him as He infuses us with His strength, so we might accomplish His good purposes because of His power at work within us.

 In what area of your life could you use a fresh infusion of spiritual strength?

 Paul's last directive? **Review 1 Corinthians 16:14**, then make a note of Paul's fifth and final command below.

Of course the last word is *love!*

How I love the word *everything*. In the original Greek it means: *each, every, any, all, the whole, everyone, all things, everything.* Yep, everything. You'll recall in yesterday's lesson, we talked about "loving everything"—from candy to coffee to club sports? Turns out that's how Paul wants the Christ followers to live. Bring those love glasses everywhere you go. Live a life of love.

I told you about Jake and me when he was at the threshold of kindergarten. Fast forward thirteen years and he was a graduated senior from high school. The stakes were now much higher as to whether or not I had done my job as a mom. John and I had just under three summer months with our boy before he went away to college, and there were countless things left to say!

We got a test run when Jake attended a one-week hockey camp in a small town in Ontario. It was only four hours away, but it seemed so strange to leave my son—the one I had watched over his whole life—on the onset of a new level of independence. It surely did not help that they housed the hockey players in a rent-by-the-week motel. There was no guardian to oversee a bunch of young athletes, no cafeteria for him to eat meals. Every guy was responsible to make their own food in the little in-room microwaves! Jake would be experiencing a level of autonomy he had never known before. (I did not clamp myself to his leg, just so you know.)

But I did wonder, "Did I as a mom do enough to prepare my beloved son to stand on his own?"

Did he pack enough Motrin in case of a muscle strain?

Would his equipment rot in his bag or would he air it out?

Would he be capable of properly nuking all the microwaveable meals that I (admittedly) purchased for him?

I fought back my urge to dispense last-minute advice about rink etiquette and wearing his neck guard. I waved him off, trying to radiate a cheer I did not totally feel. "Bye for now! Have a great time! You can do it! Love you!"

My last word to my son was *love*. Paul's was, too.

As he prepared to close his book-length letter to the Corinthians, Paul wanted to be clear: love was the lasting bond that held everything else together.

Read 1 Corinthians 16:24 and record Paul's parting words.

Paul's last word to his spiritual sons and daughters, across the ages, was love.

And God's last word to us as his precious, costly daughters is love, always love.

Apply It

Review the five directives Paul shared with this church in **1 Corinthians 16:13–14** and write them out once more. Put a heart by the one which is the easiest for you to live out. Circle the instruction which is the hardest for you to apply in your everyday life. What could you do this week to grow in this particular area?

1.

2.

3.

4.

5.

We've spent the past six weeks peeling back the pages of 1 Corinthians—a letter with a personal message from Paul to Christ followers throughout history—like you, like me.

Spend time reflecting on the lessons you've learned on your *Live Full, Walk Free* journey. Flip through your book and review your notes, discussion questions, and observations. Record a highlight from each week.

WEEK	SESSION	LIVE FULL, WALK FREE HIGHLIGHT
1	Welcome to Sin City	
2	Cliques, Fools, & Secrets	
3	New Hearts, Old Habits	
4	Sex in the Sinful City	
5	To Eat or Not to Eat	
6	Our Final Victory	

Review your challenges list on the inside back cover of your book. In what ways have you seen God work? In what areas of your life have you experienced more fullness and freedom?

 What is the one main takeaway you will leave with as we wrap up our time together in 1 Corinthians?

Video Lesson Six:
OUR FINAL VICTORY

Use the space below to note anything that stands out to you from the video lesson. You may also choose to take notes on a separate sheet of paper.

Use the following questions as a guide for group discussion:

1. What stood out to you in today's video teaching?

2. Take a look at 1 Corinthians 4:16 and 1 Corinthians 11:1. Is it arrogant for Paul to say "imitate me"? Explain. Would it be arrogant for *you* to say this? How should this affect your actions? Is there someone in your personal life you seek to "imitate" on your faith journey?

3. Review Paul's three priorities. Would you say his priorities are also your priorities? Share as you feel comfortable. Would those closest to you agree?

4. Look up 1 Corinthians 10:33 and read Paul's mission? What's your "so that"?

5. How would you answer Cindy's question, "What's the biggest obstacle for you to *live full* and *walk free*?"

Spend time in prayer asking God to remove any/all obstacles, and infuse you with fresh power *so that* you would be a mighty woman who *knows*, *lives*, and *shares* the truth everywhere she goes!

❧ Final Note from Cindy ❧

Sweet friend,

You made it to the finish line! Imagine me throwing colorful confetti as I celebrate YOU and your faithfulness to see this study through to the end. Well done!

It has been my joy and delight to journey throughout ancient Corinth with you! I'd be so honored to pray for you as we conclude our time with *Live Full, Walk Free.*

Dear God, thank You for my dear sister and the humble privilege of participating in this Live Full, Walk Free *adventure together. O Lord, how I ask that You would remind her in the deepest places of her heart and mind that she is lavishly loved by You. Please open her eyes to the purpose and plan that you have for her life. Help her to let go of anything she is holding on to that is getting in the way of the full, abundant life that You desire for her. God, I thank You that because of Jesus, we can live victoriously—regardless of being surrounded by immorality, indulgence, and idolatry. We praise You that in Christ we have a new identity: sanctified, called, enriched, and blameless. I pray that my dear friend would cling to Your truth always—including when temptation comes, old habits try to resurface, or she's faced with a sticky situation. And for all of us seeking to live set apart lives in our sin-soaked world, may we know truth, live truth, and share Your powerful truth, in love, with others everywhere we go. We love You, Lord, and we bless Your powerful and holy name. In the life-changing, delivering name of Jesus I pray. Amen.*

I would enjoy staying connected as you live out the lessons we learned in Corinth, so please keep in touch as you can. I'd love to hear from you!

With love and grace,

Memory Verse Cards

WEEK 1	WEEK 2
For the message of the cross is foolishness to those who are perishing, but to us who are being saved it is the power of God. —1 Corinthians 1:18	Do not deceive yourselves. If any of you think you are wise by the standards of this age, you should become "fools" so that you may become wise. —1 Corinthians 3:18

WEEK 3	WEEK 4
You were washed, you were sanctified, you were justified in the name of the Lord Jesus Christ and by the Spirit of our God. —1 Corinthians 6:11b	You are not your own; you were bought at a price. Therefore honor God with your bodies. —1 Corinthians 6:19b–20

WEEK 5	WEEK 6
Be careful, however, that the exercise of your rights does not become a stumbling block to the weak. —1 Corinthians 8:9	Be on your guard; stand firm in the faith; be courageous; be strong. Do everything in love. —1 Corinthians 16:13–14

1 Corinthians Reading Plan

Day 1	1:1–17	Day 13	10:1–22
Day 2	1:18–31	Day 14	10:23–33
Day 3	2:1–16	Day 15	11:1–16
Day 4	3:1–23	Day 16	11:17–34
Day 5	4:1–21	Day 17	12:1–11
Day 6	5:1–13	Day 18	12:12–31
Day 7	6:1–20	Day 19	13:1–13
Day 8	7:1–16	Day 20	14:1–25
Day 9	7:17–40	Day 21	14:26–40
Day 10	8:1–13	Day 22	15:1–34
Day 11	9:1–18	Day 23	15:35–58
Day 12	9:19–27	Day 24	16:1–24

Notes

Chapter 1

1. William Barclay, *The Letters to the Corinthians* (Louisville: Westminster John Knox, 2002), 2.

2. Ancient Corinth was one of the largest and most important cities of Greece, with a population of 90,000 in 400 BC. The Romans totally destroyed Corinth in 146 BC, built a new city in its place in 44 BC, and later made it the provincial capital of Greece.

3. Henry Blackaby, *1 Corinthians: A Blackaby Bible Study Series* (Nashville: Lifeway, 2008), 7.

4. Barclay, *The Letters to the Corinthians*, 3.

5. Paul's conversion story is found also in Acts 22:6–12 and Acts 26:12–18.

6. Kenneth E. Bailey, *Paul through Mediterranean Eyes: Cultural Studies in 1 Corinthians* (London: SPCK, 2011), 34.

7. Charles F. Pfeiffer, *The Wycliffe Bible Encyclopedia* (Chicago: Moody Press, 1990).

8. Acts 17:18.

9. 1 Corinthians 6:11.

10. 1 Corinthians 1:18 MSG.

11. Bailey, *Paul through Mediterranean Eyes*, 49.

12. The enemy may quote Scripture to distort truth or tempt us. Matthew 4:6 is a perfect example of his sneaky schemes.

13. Jim Cymbala, *Walking Out Our Faith*, http://www.brooklyntabernacle.org/media/sermons/1326.

14. F. F. Bruce, *Paul: Apostle of the Heart Set Free* (Grand Rapids: Wm. B. Eerdmans, 1977), 264.

15. Bruce Bickel and Stan Jantz, *1 & 2 Corinthians: Finding Your Unique Place in God's Plan* (Eugene, Ore.: Harvest House, 2004), 15.

16. Bailey, *Paul through Mediterranean Eyes*, 198.

17. Rachel Williams, "A Fifth of Children Have Never Received a Letter," theguardian.com.

18. A good place to look for other translations is biblegateway.com. Widely used translations include the New International Version, English Standard Version, the New Living Translation, The Message, and the Amplified Bible.

19. Bailey, *Paul through Mediterranean Eyes*, 59.

20. "What Does the Bible Say about Christian Saints? What Are Saints?" CompellingTruth.org.

Chapter 2

1. Holy Bible: New International Version (Grand Rapids: Zondervan, 2011), 1068.

2. "Rodney King," wikipedia.com.

3. John MacArthur, *The MacArthur Bible Commentary* (Nashville: Thomas Nelson, 2007), 13.

4. William MacDonald, *Believer's Bible Commentary* (Nashville: Thomas Nelson, 1995), 1751.

5. "Corrie Ten Boom Quotes," azquotes.com.

6. James Strong, *The New Strong's Expanded Exhaustive Concordance of the Bible* (Nashville: Thomas Nelson, 2010), 169. Note that unless otherwise indicated, the definitions of most or all Hebrew and Greek words in this book are from this source.

7. *Merriam-Webster Dictionary*, http://www.merriam-webster.com/dictionary/deceived.

8. Strong, 168.

9. 1 Peter 1:10–12.

10. Rick Renner, *Sparkling Gems from the Greek* (Tulsa: Teach All Nations, 2003), 856.

11. Ray C. Stedman, *Letters to a Troubled Church: 1 and 2 Corinthians* (Grand Rapids: Discovery House, 2007), 41.

12. Keith Krell, "Warning: Don't Touch the Temple! (1 Corinthians 3:16–17)," Bible.org, https://bible.org/seriespage/10-warning-don-t-touch-temple-1 -corinthians-316-17. Used with permission.

13. Philippians 2:3 MSG.

Chapter 3

1. James Strong, *The New Strong's Expanded Exhaustive Concordance of the Bible*, 268.

2. Strong, 258.

3. Gordon Franz, "Mutiny on the *HMS Corinth*," personal interview, March 2016. What a gift to travel Greece with Professor Franz!

4. *Life Application Bible: New International Version* (Wheaton: Tyndale, 1991), 2068.

5. 1 Corinthians 5:3 MSG.

6. *Vine's Expository Dictionary of New Testament Words*, http://www2.mf.no/bible/vines.html.

7. Rick Renner, *Sparkling Gems from the Greek*, 41.

8. Please know if you have experienced the pain of divorce, I am not judging you. This is "Jenna's story" and my response based on her circumstances. No judgment from me. Promise.

9. The sinful woman in Luke 7 is not the same woman recorded in Matthew 26, Mark 14, or John 12.

10. Romans 3:23 MSG.

11. Renner, 599.

Chapter 4

1. Rick Renner, *Sparkling Gems from the Greek 2* (Tulsa: Teach All Nations, 2016), 134.

2. "Talking about Sex and Puberty," *Focus on the Family*, May 2011, http://www.focusonthefamily.com/parenting/sexuality/talking-about-sex/talking-about-sex-and-puberty.

3. We talked about Jesus' message of "shame off you" in video lesson 3.

4. "End Sex Trafficking," *Equality Now*, March 3, 2016, http://www.equalitynow.org/issues/end-sex-trafficking.

5. Chip Ingram, *Culture Shock* (Grand Rapids: Baker, 2014), 60.

6. Kevin DeYoung, *The Hole in Our Holiness* (Wheaton: Crossway, 2012), 109.

7. DeYoung, 110.

8. Renner, *Sparkling Gems from the Greek 2*, 135.

9. Lysa TerKeurst, *Unglued* (Grand Rapids: Zondervan, 2012), 32–33.

10. James Strong, *The New Strong's Expanded Exhaustive Concordance of the* Bible, 169.

11. Beth Moore, *Breaking Free* (Nashville: Broadman & Holman, 2007), 245.

12. Henry Blackaby, *1 Corinthians: A Blackaby Bible Study Series*, 7.

Chapter 5

1. You can learn more about my journey through grief at www.cindybultema.com.

2. Eric Russ, "Gray Areas," *Discipleship Defined* | 2013, http://www.discipleshipdefined.com/resources/gray-areas.

3. Bob Deffinbaugh, "19. Table Talk (1 Cor. 10:14–33)," Bible.org, https://bible.org/seriespage/19-table-talk-1-cor-1014-33. Used with permission.

4. *"Proskomma," Blue Letter Bible,* https://www.blueletterbible.org.

5. Ephesians 5:18.

6. John and I are so thankful to our Greek guide, James. He was wise, personable, and oh so helpful.

7. William Greenfield, *A Greek-English Lexicon to the New Testament* (Grand Rapids: Zondervan, 1970).

8. John Piper, *Don't Waste Your Life* (Wheaton: Crossway, 2003).

9. *"Adokimos," Blue Letter Bible.*

10. 2 Timothy 1:12; Romans 8:31–39.

11. 2 Corinthians 5:10.

12. We heard Gordon live, but he shares a similar message online. Gordon Franz, "Going for the Gold: The Apostle Paul and the Isthmian Games," Associates for Biblical Research, http://www.biblearchaeology.org/post/2012/07/16/Going-for-the-Gold-The-Apostle-Paul-and-the-Isthmian-Games.aspx#Article.

Chapter 6

1. Matthew 4:1–11.

2. James Strong, *The New Strong's Expanded Exhaustive Concordance of the Bible,* 199.

3. Shared by Matt Kenney, a Christian counselor, who specializes in helping those who struggle with pornography. www.journeychristiancounseling.com.

4. Rick Renner, *Sparkling Gems from the Greek,* 617.

5. Taylor Berglund, "Pastor Perry Noble Fired After 16 Years at NewSpring Church," *Charisma News,* http://www.charismanews.com/us/58283-pastor-perry-noble-fired-after-16-years-at-newspring-church.

6. Karl Vaters, "Perry Noble, NewSpring Church, and Our Obsession with Numbers," http://www.christianitytoday.com/karl-vaters/2016/july/perry-noble-newspring-church-and-our-obsession-with-numbers.html.

7. *Merriam-Webster Dictionary.*

8. *Getting to the Heart of Conflict—Relational Wisdom | Ken Sande,* http://rw360.org/getting-to-the-heart-of-conflict/.

9. Kelly Minter, *No Other Gods* (Colorado Springs: David C. Cook, 2008).

10. "City of Brotherly Love," *The Encyclopedia of Greater Philadelphia,* philadelphiaencyclopedia.org.

11. Read about David and Jonathan's friendship in 1 Samuel 18:1–4 and 2 Samuel 1:26.

12. Rick Renner, *Sparkling Gems from the Greek*, 671.

13. "Morris Albert: Feelings," Lyric Wikia, lyrics.wikia.com.

14. Max Lucado, *A Gentle Thunder* (Nashville: Word, 1998).

15. Strong, 62.

16. *Vine's Expository Dictionary*, StudyLight.org.

17. 1 Corinthians 4:10.